HOW TO HEPBURN

HOW TO HEPBURN

LESSONS ON LIVING FROM

Kate the Great

KAREN KARBO

BLOOMSBURY

Published by Bloomsbury USA, New York
Distributed to the trade by Holtzbrinck Publishers

All papers used by Bloomsbury USA are natural, recyclable products made from
wood grown in well-managed forests. The manufacturing processes conform to
the environmental regulations of the country of origin.

LIBRARY OF CONGRESS CATALOGING-IN-PUBLICATION DATA HAS BEEN APPLIED FOR.

ISBN-10 1-59691-351-7
ISBN-13 978-1-59691-351-6

First U.S. Edition 2007

1 3 5 7 9 10 8 6 4 2

Designed by Sara Stemen

Typeset by Westchester Book Group
Printed in the United States of America by Quebecor World Fairfield

Dedicated to my friend Rebecca Schaeffer,
who loved Hepburn and was not unlike her

I have a feeling that millions of people think the following about you: she knows how she wants to live her life, she's succeeded at it, it's all worked out, she got what she wanted. And they feel you probably have some guiding principles, some secret, that, if only they knew them, they could be as successful and as content as you seem to be.

—DICK CAVETT, INTERVIEWING KATHARINE HEPBURN, 1973

CONTENTS

KATHARINE HEPBURN MOVIE TIME LINE

*(What was going on in the world while
Hepburn was hard at work in Hollywood)*

1932	**A Bill of Divorcement**	*London Philharmonic founded; construction begins on Golden Gate Bridge; vitamin D discovered; Hitler becomes German citizen*
1933	**Little Women** **Morning Glory**	*Philo Farnsworth develops electronic television; Hitler granted dictatorial powers; 21st Amendment repeals Prohibition*
1935	**Alice Adams**	*Roosevelt signs Social Security Act; Amelia Earhart becomes first person to fly solo across Pacific; Alcoholics Anonymous organized in New York*
1937	**Stage Door**	*Trotsky calls for overthrow of Stalin; Daffy Duck and Elmer J. Fudd debut; Anna Freud publishes* The Ego and the Mechanisms of Defense, *of which the first is denial; SPAM is trademarked*

1938	**Bringing Up Baby**	*Forty-hour workweek established in U.S.; 20,000 television sets in service in New York City; ballpoint pen invented*
1940	**The Philadelphia Story**	*Roosevelt elected to historic third term; Germany invades Norway, Denmark, Holland, Belgium, Luxembourg, and France; penicillin becomes first practical antibiotic*
1942	**Woman of the Year**	*First U.S. jet plane tested; murder of millions commences in Nazi gas chambers; Gandhi demands independence for India; Gandhi arrested*
1949	**Adam's Rib**	*Israel admitted into United Nations; USSR tests its first atomic bomb; George Orwell's* 1984 *published; RCA introduces 45 rpm record*
1951	**The African Queen**	*Peace treaty with Japan signed in San Francisco; 22nd Amendment limits president to two terms in office; J. D. Salinger's* Catcher in the Rye *published; color TV introduced*
1962	**Long Day's Journey into Night**	*Cuban missile crisis; John Steinbeck wins Nobel Prize for literature; thalidomide found to cause birth defects; Bob Dylan first performs "Blowin' in the Wind"*
1967	**Guess Who's Coming to Dinner**	*U.S attacks Hanoi; Billie Jean King wins nearly every tennis match in the world open*

		to women; Christiaan Barnard performs world's first heart transplant; Beatles release Sgt. Pepper's Lonely Hearts Club Band *(they hope you will enjoy the show)*
1968	**The Lion in Winter**	*Reverend Martin Luther King assassinated; Senator Robert F. Kennedy assassinated; Apollo 8 orbits the moon; figure skater Peggy Fleming wins only U.S. gold medal in Winter Olympics*
1981	**On Golden Pond**	*President Reagan shot; appearance of mysterious fatal disease that will come to be known as AIDS; Sandra Day O'Connor first woman appointed to Supreme Court; Donkey Kong video arcade game released; Katharine Hepburn wins historic fourth Best Actress Oscar*

Introduction

HER OWN THING

Katharine Hepburn was a born rabble-rouser and a reluctant cultural revolutionary, who handily redefined femininity, forced the world to ponder the meaning of marriage, and gave generations of women fresh options for surviving middle age and beyond. She burst onto the fledgling movie scene in 1932 and from then on had us all shook up. Hepburn was opinionated, reclusive, snooty, stubborn, exacting, cantankerous, kind, mean, hilarious, devious, courageous, and a good sport. She was notoriously hard-working, possessing the energy and fortitude of ten men. She was punctual. She was the opposite of frivolous. Her apparent inability to get with the ridiculous program of Hollywood, while still reaping all of Hollywood's rewards, eventually earned our respect, but only after decades of wondering what in the hell she was up to. There was no one like her.

I never knew Hepburn, but she was one of my mother's household saints. When I was small people always seemed to be accosting my mother at the A&P, touching her freckled forearm, and saying, "You must have heard this before—you look just like Katharine Hepburn."

Later, when I asked, my mom said Katharine Hepburn was a famous actress who had been beautiful in her youth and who "did her own thing," and for that my mother admired her. Like so many women of her time, my mother did not do her own thing. Her thing was subjected to the things of her children and husband. My mother was tall for the time and lanky, with auburn hair and a mass of freckles that covered her entire body. There the resemblance to Hepburn ended, but it was enough for my mother to feel a special kinship with her.

Aside from this, I didn't give Hepburn much thought until the early eighties, when I was accepted into the M.F.A. program at USC's School of Cinema-Television and became acquainted with the glamorous black-and-white Katharine Hepburn. Along with my classmates I rediscovered her offbeat movies from the thirties— *Christopher Strong, Holiday*, and the magnificently campy *Sylvia Scarlett*. My Katharine Hepburn was different from my mother's. She was young, exotic in her strangeness, a confirmed tomboy, a convincing cross-dresser, the Hepburn who was yet to be tamed and legitimized by her love for Spencer Tracy. A research paper I wrote called "The Role of Anarchy in 'Bringing Up Baby'" earned me an A, and a date with the biggest film nerd in the program; he was French and thought Hepburn was a genius.

In 1978, the critic Judith Crist noticed that Hepburn was not simply an actress, but an inspiration. "I can think of few actresses who served, as Hepburn has, as 'role model' for so many of us. Part tomboy, part romantic, part poet, her beauty so ingrained that it has always gone against the fashion, her spirit so valiant that it has always implied defiance of convention . . ."

While Hepburn had a deserved reputation for being compulsively instructive—she told everyone what to do, from her housekeeper to whoever was directing her current picture—the lessons she would choose to press on us aren't necessarily the most useful ones to be gleaned from examining her life. In addition to Hepburn's basic advice, her way of being, choices, and behavior also provide object lessons and what I think of as reverse object lessons. Example: Hepburn was a true and glorious redhead who never wore a lick of sunscreen and man, did she suffer the consequences.

Of course, teasing the lessons out is an inexact science. Hepburn's life can be—and has been—viewed through the prisms of a handful of excellent biographers, who've all come to disparate conclusions. There was her real life, much of which she managed to keep maddeningly private; the many legends of her life; the inaccuracies contributed by the media, which she encouraged; and the way her screen roles did or did not reflect her essential nature. Like ogres and onions, her life had layers upon layers.

Our interest in Hepburn endures because we can't quite see how she pulled it off so well for so long. Her life is one long sleight of hand. How did she do it? How did she continue to live on her own terms? How did she parlay her unusual looks into the gold standard for contemporary beauty? How did she stay relevant for so long? How did she continue, despite setbacks, to come out on top? How did she create a life story so enduring that I can turn her last name into a verb and everyone gets it? How did she—and how can we—Hepburn?

1

THE IMPORTANCE OF BEING BRASH

Hepburn Arrives in Los Angeles, Begins Irritating Everyone Immediately;
A Sampling of Brash Acts; The Pants-Wearing as an Ongoing Display of
Brashitude; Some Family History; Hepburn Is Mistaken for an Heiress;
The Ways of the Brash; What $13,675.75 Can Buy You

So much has been made about Katharine Hepburn's lifelong devotion to trousers it's of interest to note that when she
stepped off the train in Pasadena on July 4, 1932, to star in her first
movie, *A Bill of Divorcement*, she was wearing couture. A real
getup, bold and brash, "piss-elegant," as she would remember it
in *Me: Stories of My Life*, her 1991 autobiography. New York's most
expensive designer had concocted a costume for Hepburn's self-
styled grand arrival made of gray-blue grosgrain silk. The skirt was
ankle length and flared, the coat was thigh length, long and close
fitting, appropriate for a fox hunt, perhaps, but not for arriving in
Southern California in the middle of summer. "The hat was a sort
of gray-blue straw dish upside down on my head," Hepburn would
recall decades later.

The temperature upon her arrival was in the mid-nineties. During the long train trip across country some steel shavings had found their way into her eye, causing both eyes, for some reason, to turn red. She looked somewhat patriotic in her gray-blue gros-grain suit, her navy blue bag, shoes, and gloves, and her bloodshot eyes. To Leland Hayward, her agent and future paramour, waiting at the train station to collect her, she looked like a cadaver with a drinking problem.

They repaired to RKO, where Hepburn demanded to see a doctor immediately.

George Cukor, the young director who would become famous for coaxing nuanced performances out of the greatest stars of Hollywood's Golden Age, was unimpressed with his new star's ocular difficulties. He was too distracted by her strange ensemble. This was Los Angeles in the olden days, after all, when there were only orange groves and no high fashion to speak of. Cukor, no slouch when it came to reading people, could tell Hepburn thought she was the walking definition of chic, when actually the whole outfit was hideous—did I mention the ruffled turtleneck?

The doctor could wait. Cukor was eager to engage this odd girl, with her stringy, scraped-back red hair, riot of freckles, and ridiculous braying voice. He decided to show her some preliminary costume sketches. In his experience actresses always had intriguing opinions about their costumes.

—•—

Now, put yourself in Hepburn's position. You're twenty-five years old, in Los Angeles for the first time to star in your first movie. Your wily agent has negotiated $1,500 a week for you (adjusting for inflation, that's about $20,000) based solely on how you looked in a gladiator miniskirt with a dead stag balanced on your shoulders in a recent play called *The Warrior's Husband*. There was some acting involved on your part, in the starring role of Antiope, but what bowled people over were your legs, and your ability to balance a carcass on your shoulders.

You have not just ended a successful run as Lady Macbeth. You have not just won a Tony (the awards weren't founded until 1947, but you get the idea). You have played a few roles here and there, but mostly you've gotten fired for shooting your mouth off. Furthermore, you're not conventionally pretty. Indeed, many theater producers, directors, and impresarios think you're a freak. You live during a time when the height of feminine beauty was five foot two, eyes of blue, coochie-coochie-coochie-coo. You have the requisite blue eyes, but that's it. You're a gangling five feet seven inches, give or take, and anyone who'd try to coochie you would soon be in search of a raw steak for his black eye. You're called, variously, "a cross between a monkey and a horse" and "a boa constrictor on a fast." Decades down the road no aspiring actress will have a snowball's chance of landing a leading role if she *doesn't* look like a boa constrictor on a fast, but in 1932 the world preferred women who could not be mistaken for war orphans.

Not only is there not much, experience-wise, to have justified landing this plum role, opposite the great John Barrymore, but you are making more than Cukor, the director, who just came off directing a picture with French heartthrob Maurice Chevalier.

The Great Depression is just getting into full swing, and there's famine in Russia (you come from an educated, socially progressive family, so presumably you would know, and might even care, about these things); your $1,500 a week could probably feed a family of six for as many years. There has already been talk that you're making far more than you're worth. In some respected corners of Hollywood, people don't think you're worth $500 a week; they don't think you're worth $5 a week.

Also, if you were to be honest with yourself (not always your strong suit), you don't think you're a born actress. You possess heat and flair, but your first stage performances were catastrophic. You get nervous, which causes your buzz saw of a voice to go high and scratchy. One was reminded of courting cats on a fence at two A.M. You know, somewhere inside, that it will take years of effort and discipline to refine and develop what talent you truly possess. You will have to work and work.

You are dying to be a famous actress. Nothing else has captured your imagination like this. *A Bill of Divorcement* is *it*, your big break. Being aware of all this, wouldn't you be a smidge deferential when presented with your character's costume sketches by the movie's esteemed director? Especially since you've been in the man's presence for all of about ninety minutes, and you're somewhat interested in his not thinking you're a castrating bitch, or whatever they called it in 1932?

Or, if not deferential—after all, you are on the way to becoming one of the greatest stars in cinematic history, so perhaps it's impossible—at least noncommittal? Maybe you'd say, "Hmmm, interesting," or even, "I could see how that would be absolutely stunning on a different kind of girl." You would be polite. You would be nice.

But Hepburn was Hepburn, even then. She was one of the Brash. She harrumphed, folded her skinny arms over her skinny chest, and probably literally and not figuratively turned up her nose. She said, in that snooty buzz-saw Bryn Mawr voice, that *she* didn't think any proper English girl would be caught dead in that sort of ensemble, and why hadn't the studio rounded up Chanel to do the costumes?

Cukor said, "Considering the way you look, I can hardly take your judgment seriously."

The dialogue flew back and forth. Like many famous seventy-five-year-old Hollywood anecdotes, over the years this one has taken on the flavor of a screwball comedy in which she said she thought she looked quite smart, and he said he thought she looked idiotic. Hepburn and Cukor groused at one another a bit, but in the end it was the beginning of a half-century-long friendship.

Years later Cukor would say that he accepted Hepburn's attitude as part of her supreme self-assurance. Not only did he *not* hold it against her, he thought her attitude was a point in her favor. So unaffected was he by her brashness, after they quibbled about the sketches he gave her over to the makeup department, where they cut her long, stringy red hair (she did not have terrific

hair) into a bob, which made it look lustrous and thick, and covered her blotchy, freckly face with Pan-Cake makeup (she did not
have terrific skin), both of which served to emphasize her sensational bone structure, the most fabulous bone structure in the
history of cinema, up to and including the one belonging to
Johnny Depp.

—◆—

According to the Merriam-Webster dictionary, *brash* is defined as
"audacious" (a *brash* adventurer); someone or something "full of a
fresh raw vitality" (a *brash* frontier town) or who is "uninhibitedly
energetic" (a *brash* comedian). Brashness has several negative con-
notations as well. It's also defined as "tactless" (*brash* remarks) and
"aggressively self-assertive" (*brash* to the point of arrogance).

A sampling of Hepburn's acts of brashness might include:

- Skinny-dipping in the library cloister fountain at Bryn Mawr
  in the early-morning hours to "refresh" herself after having
  studied all night; around the same time she also conned a
  friend in her dorm into photographing her naked, in order to
  watch the pharmacist at the local drugstore squirm when
  asked to develop the film.

- Stealing the script for *Morning Glory* off the desk of producer
  Pandro Berman. Hepburn was convinced the starring role,

written by Zoe Akins for Constance Bennett, was for her. Despite the thievery, Hepburn strong-armed Berman into agreeing with her and went on to win her first Oscar.

o Successfully buying herself out of several professional contracts, which encouraged her to try to buy Mary Ford (for $150,000) out of her marriage to director John Ford, with whom Hepburn had fallen in love during the filming of *Mary of Scotland*. The story is apocryphal, but is too believable to fall out of circulation.

o Disobeying the Bel Air Country Club's rules against women playing on Sundays.

o Sneaking out of UCLA Medical Center at four o'clock one morning after secret hip-replacement surgery.

By the time Hepburn underwent her hip replacement it was 1974, and this was considered vintage Hepburn behavior. No one expected anything less of her. Hepburn simply wasn't Hepburn if she wasn't outspoken and bullheaded. Her audacity had become a trademark; it had been codified. If there is a lesson here, it's this: people are not as put off by bold behavior as we might imagine.

◆—◆—◆

A Bill of Divorcement was made a scant three years after motion pictures acquired sound, which in those days meant one dialogue track and one music track.* It would be some time before you would hear a door open and close, a chair scrape back, cutlery dropped on a plate, or even footsteps. Despite its primitive production values, the movie is still watchable, primarily for the fresh joy of seeing Katharine before she became Hepburn.

John Barrymore is Hilary Fairfield, who escapes from an asylum, where he's been locked up for a few decades due, apparently, to a bad case of shell shock suffered during the First World War. Meanwhile, his wife, Meg (Billie Burke, embedded in the psyche of millions of us as the nicest person ever, Glinda the Good Witch), has obtained the titular divorce, in order to remarry. Their daughter, Sydney (Hepburn), is desperately in love and also planning to marry when Hilary shows up in the living room, and it's revealed that his shell shock is really a species of insanity that runs in the family. Naturally, this means Sydney must dump her fiancé for fear of passing on her tainted genes and resign herself to caring for her demented father for the rest of her life.

The movie can be read as a primer on Hepburn's personality. Her brashness gives her the air of a horse that's just been broke. She's breathtaking in the scenes conveying a sense of fun and high jinks; convincingly tactless and bold in delivering her unsolicited opinions; utterly believable when she melodramatically decides to

---

*If a *A Bill of Divorcement* was remade today, the sound would comprise about fifty separate tracks of dialogue, music, background effects, and special effects.

give up her entire future to tend to her father (and, as the film ends, help him complete his wretched half-finished sonata). The standard love scenes, in which she lies nestled in the arms of her fiancé as they cutely discuss all the children they're going to have, are cringe-worthy; an aspiring twelve-year-old actress appearing in her middle school's production of *Grease* could play a more convincing fool in love.

Critics and audiences adored Sydney's brashness, imagining it was the brashness of youth Hepburn was so adept at portraying, when, in fact, it was simply Hepburn's own brand of brashness, which she would never outgrow and which would cause her no end of trouble.

◆—◆—◆

Undoubtedly some graduate student somewhere has written a master's thesis about Katharine Hepburn and her pants. Hepburn's trousers were customarily cotton and loose-fitting. She wore them with sneakers or loafers and white socks, or sandals with a thick strap and a solid heel. One Hollywood columnist reported that Hepburn not infrequently showed up on the set looking like a Mexican ski-jumper. When she began making real money, she hired a men's tailor to make custom-fitted suits.

Once, she wore jeans to work. That was simply too much. In the 1930s, no one wore jeans but farmers, forty-niners, and movie cowboys. A production assistant was instructed to take Hepburn's jeans while she was in her dressing room, hoping to shame her into finding a skirt to slip into. Instead, Hepburn traipsed around in her underwear until the jeans were returned.

The graduate student is probably ahead of me in supposing that the pants were a symbolic representation of Hepburn's brashness, a handy stand-in for her outrageous behavior, so that even while she was on the set reading a book or knitting a sweater, or otherwise minding her own business, her wearing trousers set her apart from all the other ladies in the vicinity, who were imprisoned in a dress, and the requisite slip, girdle, garter belt, stockings, and high heels.

Over the years, Hepburn floated various explanations for the pants. She said she couldn't bear the thought of wearing stockings — an article of clothing designed by the devil — or, she claimed, she didn't like heels, and you couldn't wear a skirt with flats, because it looked too ridiculous (more ridiculous than a Mexican ski-jumper, apparently).

Most often, she said it was a basic issue of comfort. It's difficult to imagine the chronic low-grade scandal this attitude caused at the time. In the 1930s, dress-wearing was expected, even in the notoriously freewheeling film business. Imagine a modern college girl showing up to Sunday dinner at her grandma's (does such a thing still exist?) in the orange short shorts and white tank top she wears to work at Hooters and you have a rough idea how much consternation and disapproval were generated by Hepburn's wandering the world in slacks.

Hepburn's devotion to trousers was bred in the bone. In her tomboy youth she was routinely sent home from grade school for showing up in her older brother Tom's hand-me-downs. Her mother, unimpressed with dress codes, would send Kath straight back to school.

Nothing changed when Hepburn arrived at Bryn Mawr. Actually, not true. There was a much reported moment early in her freshman year when she showed up for dinner properly outfitted in a blue skirt and sweater and was mocked by an upperclassman who said something along the lines of "Ah! Conscious beauty!"

Hepburn fled, humiliated, and ate in her room for the rest of the term. For the rest of her life, dresses were costumes she'd don only when the spirit infrequently moved her. By her junior year, Hepburn's pants had become her trademark. She was the first girl on record to wear pants to class. Her baggies were so raggedy she held them up with safety pins, a style that, when combined with Hepburn's devotion to the pursuit of fun (smoking; skinny-dipping in the library fountain; breaking and entering), could best be described as Hobo Flapper.

You'd think that once Hepburn graduated and set out upon her professed career path as world-famous actress, she would rethink her look. You'd think she'd check out the Bernard-Hewitt & Co. Summer 1928 Apparel Catalog, printed around the time Hepburn presented herself to theater impresario Edwin H. Knopf (brother of New York publisher Alfred), and perhaps spring for a nice drop-waisted frock. For $1, she could have purchased a smartly styled voile dress with knife-pleated skirt, three-quarter sleeves, wide sash, and "streamer at back."

Instead, she appeared in baggy slacks and jacket, no makeup, hair stuck up in the charwoman's bun that would become her trademark. There are conflicting accounts, but she may also have been wearing a felt hat with a hole in it.

She handed Knopf a letter of introduction from the friend of a college friend. While he read it, she stood clenching and unclenching her hands, her freckled face blotchy from nerves, sweating like a boiler repairman. Just because she was brash, that doesn't mean she wasn't a wreck. Knopf, recalling the moment much later, said, "She was awkward, green, freaky-looking. I wanted no part of her."

And yet, she wound up getting the job anyway.

❧

Being brash can be nurtured, but it helps if you are born to a pair of bossy, assertive parents. The Brash among us tend to be homozygous for brashitude. Katharine Houghton and Thomas Norval Hepburn, known by their Hemingwayesque nicknames Kit and Hep, were insufferably bold and proud of it. Kit, a suffragette and birth-control advocate who helped found the organization that would become Planned Parenthood, was brilliant, valiant, erudite, and loving. Hep, a urologist who crusaded against venereal disease and corresponded passionately on the matter for a time with George Bernard Shaw, was brilliant, exacting, athletic, and sort of mean and withholding by contemporary standards.

Both were largely self-made. Hep's people hailed from Virginia, where they lost everything in the Civil War. His father, Sewell (from whom Kate inherited her essential tremor), was a country preacher.

Hep would become one of Hartford, Connecticut's most respected urologists, but he had to build his practice from the ground up, like any doctor starting out.

Kit was a Houghton, whose family founded the Corning Glass Works, the world's then-leading manufacturer of lightbulbs. They also counted among their number a bunch of ambassadors and the founder of Houghton Mifflin. As a young woman Kit traded on this association, although she was from the side of the family that caused anguish and shame, that was poor and prone to suicide. It was Kit's uncle, Amory Houghton, who was the great success; Kit's father, Alfred, killed himself when Kit was small, and her mother died of stomach cancer shortly thereafter, leaving Kit, sixteen, alone with her two younger sisters.

It fell on Amory to decide what to do with these leftover females. He farmed the girls out to another family member, who presented the girls with a monthly bill for their upkeep, which included a charge for bathwater. Still, Kit swallowed her pride and allowed her loathsome uncle, who was nevertheless brilliant with money, to invest the pittance she'd inherited from her mother. Amory thought Kit was stupid and profligate and was against education for women in general; still Kit bided her time and eventually used the profits of her investments to send herself (and eventually her sisters) to Bryn Mawr, where she allowed everyone to think she was one of the Corning Houghtons—rich and entitled—instead of the crafty poseur she was. Anyone who wants to know where Hepburn got her chutzpah need look no further than her mother.

Brashness was a way of life for Kit and Hep. They were consumed by their radical social causes. They were passionate and uninhibited. No topics of conversation were off-limits. At dinner they would merrily chat about the scourge of gonorrhea over the soup course, daring the good families of Hartford—not known as a hotbed of freethinkers—to brand them as kooks. And so they were, as were their six children, Tom, Kath, Dick, Bob, Marion, and Peg, who were allowed to be seen, heard, and often viewed swinging from the neighborhood trees. The children were ostracized. It was them against the world, a lifelong habit Hepburn was happy to embrace. "Being loved can be so demoralizing," she once quipped. She was proud of the chip on her shoulder.

Well into her dotage Hepburn still recalled the neighbor with the fancy limousine who would dispatch the car to pick up all the kids on her block for parties and dances, taking special care to exclude Hepburn. The neighbor liked to say, "That Hepburn child is always flying about on that bicycle. She can come on it."

Hepburn was further set apart from her peers when, just shy of fourteen, she found her fifteen-year-old brother, Tom, hanging by a noose styled from torn bedsheets. Tom was dutiful, smart, and athletic enough to please Hep, who made it a house rule to excel in sports. From the time his sister Kathy was born, he was devoted to her. On the first day of kindergarten it was Tom, and not Kit, who walked Kathy the mile to school.

In the hours after Kathy found him, there seemed to be no question that Tom had hanged himself. Immediately after his son's death, Hep issued a statement saying that the boy must have experienced a brief bout of insanity. There could be no other explanation. But then Kathy, who couldn't bear to see her father anguished and distraught, took matters into her own hands. She suggested that perhaps it was not a suicide, but a stunt gone wrong, that Tom was practicing a fake-hanging trick to scare them.

Another family might have dismissed the girl as too shocked to accept the truth or chided her for inventing things or for sticking her nose into serious grown-up business. Instead, Hep latched onto this explanation—of course! A stunt!—and went so far as to reissue a statement to the papers, apologizing to his deceased son for impugning his good name. It was a horrible practical joke, a boyish prank gone wrong.

Even at the end of her life Hepburn could not bear to admit Tom had committed suicide. In her autobiography she keeps the possibility open that it was an accident and not the far-fetched explanation she helped her beloved dad concoct so that no one would have to face the truth. Throughout her life, Hepburn's boldness helped her rewrite history without losing a wink.

◆—◆—◆

By the time Hepburn won her first Oscar in 1934, for her role as Eva Lovelace, the charming and deluded aspiring actress in *Morning Glory*, the world assumed Hepburn was a madcap heiress from the East. The RKO publicity department pushed the story upon the gullible public, and Hepburn's Bryn Mawr accent, equine looks, haughty demeanor, and boyish stride* provided hard evidence; Hepburn looked the part. It didn't hurt matters that she'd also arrived in L.A. with Laura Harding, the genuine heiress article, and that together they tooled around town in their ostentatious rented Hispano-Suiza roadster, with its enormous silver hood ornament and gleaming fenders, and behaved as if Hollywood were beneath them.

Of course Hepburn was merely an upper-middle-class WASP; privileged by any standards, but not living-off-the-interest wealthy. In her brashness she'd figured out how to mimic the bearing of an aristocrat—shades of her mother's own days at Bryn Mawr—and became justifiably famous for playing several of them. The Hepburns were good old penny-pinching Yankees, who drove their cars until they broke down by the side of the road and thought any man with more than two suits was a dandy, and not to be trusted. Hepburn was not heir to untold wealth, but to some fine traditions and values—including the sort of brashness that would allow her to pass herself off as an heiress.

—•—

As important as it is in life to cultivate brashness, it's not a trait easily cultivated. It helps if you also possess charisma, but it's not necessary. The sheer act of acting brash conveys your belief in

---

*Appropriated from It girl and New York socialite Hope Williams, who'd starred in *Holiday* on Broadway, and to whom Hepburn had served as an understudy for many months.

the power of your own charm, not unlike a pure bluff in poker.

Then, and now, it's risky behavior. Young women are permitted to be brash if they're also devastatingly sexy. If stilettos and something vaguely pornographic are involved, then brashness is permitted, but only just. At first, Hepburn was made to pay for her brashness. She was flat out fired from the Broadway production of Philip Barry's *The Animal Kingdom* for being, as costar Leslie Howard called her, "that irritating girl." Later, Hepburn would say that Howard wanted her fired because she towered over him; in fact, he was four inches taller than she.

Garden-variety bossiness, in which a woman heeds the siren song of her own opinions and doesn't much care what anyone else thinks—thereby making her difficult to get along with—is still frowned upon. It's never been terribly stylish, but some decades are better for opinionated women than others. Still, since the dawn of time, if a person didn't make a fuss about things, she risked getting walked on. The sad truth is that being nice and accommodating rarely results in praise for those qualities; rather they are a signal to the not-nice and the unaccommodating that you won't give them any trouble.

In an interview with Rex Reed, Hepburn once said, apropos her brashness, "I had to [behave that way] or they would have had me playing whores or discontented wives who always wonder whether they should go to bed with some bore."

Fortunately, brashness is not unlike cooking with saffron: a little goes a long way.

If you are to be brash, consider:

Confidence Is More Important than Knowledge

This is usually easier to pull off when you are very young and already know everything anyway. The day Kate Hepburn graduated from Bryn Mawr, she informed her parents on the trip home that she was going to be a famous movie actress. They were appalled. In those days acting was thought to be indulgent, silly, and superficial. It was the career choice of show-offs and would-be streetwalkers. Kit was a little less censorious, thinking perhaps her daughter might find her way to performing Shakespeare and Bernard Shaw (her favorite playwright and Hep's acquaintance), but a career as a movie queen in Hollywood? Dear Lord.

The degree to which Hepburn had absolutely no idea what she was getting into, nor even any idea what she was talking about, cannot be underestimated. The extent of her experience was a love of cowboy movies and the few plays she'd participated in at Bryn Mawr. As Hepburn admitted throughout her life—so boldly it sounded as if she were being facetious—she just wanted to be famous. It was an ambition no more elevated than that of any unimaginative seventh-grader who longs to be an international rock diva.

The Brash Are Not Afraid to Grandstand a Little

To be brash means to be no stranger to the grand gesture. It acknowledges the theatricality of the behavior. To go on a secret shopping spree and buy ten cashmere turtlenecks when one will do may be impulsive, but it is not brash.

In the fall of 1940 Franklin Roosevelt, running for an unprecedented third term, invited a group of artists to lunch at his Hyde Park estate. Travel arrangements were made to ferry the guests to the Hudson Valley from Manhattan. Hepburn spurned the group travel plans, choosing instead to rent a seaplane, which brought her straight from her family summer house, Fenwick, located on the spit of sand where the Connecticut River meets Long Island Sound (the original shingled Victorian was destroyed in the hurricane of 1938; the family immediately rebuilt what they hoped was a stronger structure, which stands to this day). The plane touched down on the Hudson, Hepburn rolled up her khakis, hopped out, and waded through the river sludge to shore, shouting to Mrs. Roosevelt, "Hey, is this the Roosevelt place?"

The Brash Think Nothing of Eating a Little Humble Pie

Just because you're brash doesn't mean you don't make mistakes. To be brash means to be able to accept bad choices and missteps. As Reggie Jackson said, "Home run hitters strike out a lot." Hepburn appeared in a lot of wretched movies that even the geekiest of film students would never embrace. Of her fifty-two films, more than half are mediocre, and some are plain awful. Hepburn spared herself the humiliation by watching very few of them.

In 1928, during the seemingly endless months Hepburn understudied Hope Williams in *Holiday*, Williams could smell Hepburn's ambition and made it her business never to get sick and give Hepburn her chance. During the show's entire run, Williams avoided catching even the sniffles. Hepburn grew mad with impatience.

This wasn't the acting life! She quit and immediately took her beau, Ludlow Ogden Smith, up on his offer of marriage. They were wed on December 12. Hepburn's grandfather Sewell officiated. She was twenty-one. She resolved to give up the theater and become a Main Line Philadelphia housewife. After two weeks of desultory house hunting she fled to the theater to beg for her job back. Was Hepburn embarrassed to come crawling back? No one knows; to be brash means either to be beyond embarrassment or good at hiding it.

If You Obey All the Rules, You Miss All the Fun

The Brash are not anarchists. The Brash don't believe in breaking rules simply for the fun of breaking them (well, maybe a little).

A short list of rules Hepburn did not obey:

1. The pants, the pants, the pants
2. If she lost a button, she replaced it with a large safety pin
3. She didn't wear makeup
4. She didn't attend Hollywood parties
5. While other actors, producers, and directors were attending Hollywood parties, she would sometimes break into their houses, just to have a look around
6. She did all her own stunts
7. She refused to autograph pictures (although she would answer fan mail)
8. She was a lesbian (unconfirmed)
9. She was bisexual (unconfirmed)

10. Spencer Tracy, a married man, was the love of her life (confirmed)
11. She kept her private life private (i.e., she never treated her personal affairs as currency)
12. She was opinionated, but not in a spunky, amusing way; it got on everyone's nerves
13. She refused to allow men to tell her what to do

Money Spent to Secure Your Freedom Is Money Well Spent
The Frugal would give you an argument on this one, and it's rather amazing that the prudent Hep and Kit didn't manage to talk their more profligate daughter out of spending her hard-earned money on what amounted to extortion. In 1934 Jed Harris directed Kate in *The Lake,* arguably the worst stage performance in Hepburn's incredibly long life (forty-seven years later The Thespian Who Wouldn't Die would turn in a Tony-nomination-worthy performance in *The West Side Waltz*).

The Lake was a British import in which Hepburn played Stella, a spoiled rich girl who dallies out of boredom with a married neighbor, agrees to marry some random suitor she doesn't love to save herself from her bad behavior, then realizes maybe she *does* love her new husband after all, only to have him die tragically in a car crash. One can imagine the many opportunities for overacting.

Harris was universally disliked, was said to be Disney's inspiration for the Big Bad Wolf. My, what big teeth he had: even though Hepburn's performance was god-awful, he refused to let her out of her agreement to tour with the production, as was common in those days.*

Hepburn knew she was bad, and Harris reminded her she was bad every chance he got; still, in a mere fifteen months Katharine Hepburn had gone from boa constrictor on a fast to a Big Movie Star, and Harris was determined not to squander her star power, insisting she go on the road so he could cash in. Hepburn begged to be let off the hook. Harris was having none of it, until Hepburn said she'd give him every penny she had. He laughed and accepted her offer.

The amount in her account? $13,675.75. According to NASA's Computer Price Index, this equals $192,787.05 in 2004 dollars. Tom's Inflation Calculator puts the amount at $205,572.61 in 2006.

If dropping this much money to secure her freedom gave Hepburn heart failure, there is no record of it. I suspect, in the manner of one born Brash, she moved right on without giving it another thought.

---

*When a show tours today, the actor who originated the role is always replaced by one of the stars of *Who's the Boss?*, determined to make a comeback.

2

STRIVE TO DEFY CATEGORIZATION

*Hepburn Redefines Femininity, and Just About Everything Else; Katharine
Hepburn Is Not a Man; Brand Kate; A Few of Hepburn's Eccentricities;
The Three Ages of Women in Hollywood; The Counterculture
Embraces Hepburn, Much to Her Chagrin*

⸻ ◆ ⸻

Talking about Hepburn's life also means talking about the *idea*
of Hepburn's life. There is the life she led, the life she wanted
us to think she led, and the life we want to believe she led. Our entire perception of the lady strains the limits of postmodernism.
Hepburn managed to elude almost all categorizations during her
lifetime. So successfully did she refuse to be pinned down, she was
the lone individual belonging to the genus *Hepburnius*.

Her greatest achievement was a complete overhaul of traditional notions of femininity. She told Dick Cavett, during that
historic 1973 interview, that among her siblings "she was the
missing link." She wasn't as eccentric as they were (one finds this
hard to believe), but she was something altogether new; a new sort
of woman.

It is thus with great regret that I must call the esteemed biographer William Mann, author of the recent *Kate: The Woman Who Was Hepburn*, on his gender imperialism. Because Hepburn was courageous, driven, hardheaded, and fair; because she was independent, able to compartmentalize, and adored golf; Mr. Mann, who wrote an otherwise sensational and nuanced biography, wants to claim her for his team. He would like us to believe she was really a man stuck in a woman's body, otherwise known in these modern times as transgendered, defined by the *Random House Unabridged Dictionary* as "appearing or attempting to be a member of the opposite sex, as a transsexual or habitual cross-dresser."

That is simply not very sporting of Mr. Mann. It brings to mind an old joke whose provenance I can't recall about how it was really a woman who discovered fire, and a man just hit her over the head with his club and stole it.

Hepburn was a woman, albeit an androgynous one. She respected masculinity, and it's true she was bold as brass, but she also loved to cook, gossip, decorate, take care of people, and submit herself to difficult men with drinking problems. What to make of those feminine qualities?

Mr. Mann's argument for Hepburn's manhood rests on Hepburn's creation of "Jimmy," the male alter ego she invented at age ten. Not having grown up female, Mr. Mann did not get the memo that pretty much every girl who doesn't want to be a princess—that most girly-girl of aspirations—has a male alter ego.

Hepburn—like many of her fellow enduring cultural icons—is a walking Rorschach test for the times. Whatever is most true in general about our cultural attitudes is projected onto the life of the icon. One can easily see this in the matter of Hepburn's sexuality (which eventually led to questions about her gender).

When the world got the first whiff of something extramarital going on between Hepburn and Tracy in the early sixties (you will remember the famous *Look* magazine interview with Tracy in which he referred to Hepburn as "my Kate"), we lauded her for her terrific sense of discretion, her refusal to break up the Tracy family, her humble acceptance of her role as mistress-in-the-shadows. The world perceived and accepted her as a sort of second wife, because she was so well-behaved. People felt sorry for her because she and Spencer could never marry.

In the seventies and eighties, when playing around became slightly less scandalous and divorce rates rose, the world had less need to cast her in the role of second fiddle to Mrs. Tracy and was more impressed that she and Spence stuck it out for twenty-five-plus years. No one else was managing to stay married for twenty-five months, much less twenty-five years. What fidelity! What loyalty!

Beginning around the time Rock Hudson issued his poignant press release in 1985 telling the world he was dying of AIDS, we became concerned with who in Hollywood might be zooming a member of the same sex. The word *gaydar* officially entered the language in 1992, and many of us aimed ours in the direction of just about everyone who's ever starred in a Hollywood movie. If Rock Hudson was gay, what did that make Cary Grant? What did that make Burt Reynolds? Harrison Ford? Tom Cruise, about whom people still feel weirdly compelled to crack the obligatory gay joke (really, there ought to be a statute of limitations)? Jake Gyllenhaal and Heath Ledger cannot possibly be gay, or else they would never have starred in *Brokeback Mountain*, or so the conventional wisdom goes. Of course, any actress who ever looked terrific in a pair of slacks and isn't a total idiot was presumed to be lesbian. Hepburn was particularly suspect because she "never married" (her marriage to Luddy was discounted).

One theory is that Laura Harding was the true love of Hepburn's life, even though the 1930s equivalent of stumbling upon them in flagrante in the backyard hot tub never occurred. Biographers have their suspicions, but mostly they have Hepburn wearing trousers and doing her own stunts and refusing to marry Howard Hughes. They have circumstantial evidence (once Harding jokingly referred to herself as Hepburn's husband. Aha! Proof!).

Still, we live in an age where we are determined to believe that *something* was going on. It is impossible to imagine a star of Hepburn's magnitude living a life more or less nooky-free. We refuse to believe that someone so famous could have other things to do. But consider: The woman's schedule was punishing. She worked twelve-hour days, six days a week, rising every day before dawn for a swim or a tennis lesson. If Laura Harding *were* Hepburn's husband, people would assume they'd barely have the energy for a bit of desultory marital cuddling, much less all the chandelier-swinging we imagine went on between her and her gal pal.

Director John Ford once called Hepburn "half-Puritan, half-Pagan," but what if it was more like seventy percent Puritan? A few puritanical things we know about Hepburn for sure: she made a religion out of cold showers, eating a stewed fruit with dinner, and turning in while it was practically still light outside. The most radical, and thus unimaginable, notion is that a movie star—or anyone, really—can take sex or leave it, that she might be more interested in her work, or her golf game, than in canoodling with men or women. Still, there can be no glamour without illicit sex, and so we will continue to speculate.

Transgendered is to the new millennium what homosexuality was to the late-twentieth century. Now that prime-time television shows think nothing of showing two attractive women French-kissing, being thought gay, or actually being gay, is old hat. (It must be said that this ho-hum sense of acceptance applies to women and not men. Male homosexuality is still outré.)

Now, however, the cutting edge of gender politics is being transgendered. We need look no further than the trend-sensitive soap opera *All My Children*, which has recently introduced a character named Zarf, a woman in a man's body who makes the gender transition accordingly. The same month this new story line was announced, New York City's Board of Health considered a proposal to allow people to change their gender on their birth certificate to reflect the gender they felt themselves to be, aside from anatomical reality.

I refuse to accept that Katharine is truly Jimmy. When I was eight, I re-created myself as Spike, an aspiring Formula One race-car driver, whom I blame for this refusal to tolerate Mr. Mann's perspective. Spike was typical boy—unthinking, hyperactive, prone toward breaking bones, a practical joker. He thinks Kate is just a girl in trousers.

In the interest of allowing everyone to make up his or her own mind, however, Karen, who sadly possesses few of Hepburn's stellar male traits, who is resolutely a woman in a woman's body, feels obliged to present several schools of thought regarding Hepburn's true gender identity:

a) Hepburn was a man in a woman's body, i.e., transgendered. All the things we admire about her character—her vigor, her energy, her forthrightness, her courage—are male traits, which no woman could possibly hope to possess. This also speaks to her penchant for wearing pants; if she were a proper woman, she would have chosen a life of perpetual discomfort in a skirt, girdle, stockings, and heels. It was Jimmy, not Kate, who said stockings were the invention of the devil.

b) Hepburn was a woman in a woman's body, albeit a woman so ahead of her time, no one knew what to make of her. Her modernity was reflected in her androgyny. She was leaps and bounds ahead of the rest of us on the evolutionary scale. Without Hepburn, there could have been no Madonna, or Trinity, from the *Matrix* trilogy, or any female characters who kick some serious ass. She made pants for women acceptable. She helped pave the way for the blue jeans revolution. In 1986 she won a lifetime achievement award from the Council of Fashion Designers, about which she said, "We're in a pretty serious spot when the original bag lady wins a prize for the way she looks."

c) Hepburn defies easy categorization.

◆—◆

Before dispensing with this topic, I'd like to take issue with one of Hepburn's oft-quoted remarks that seems so subversive and sassy, but which I feel obliged to point out makes little sense. Many times she said, "I've lived life like a man!" What "man" is she referring to, do you think? Most of the men she must have known in her prime were oft-married, usually with a mistress or three on the side. Children issued from the various marriages, and various wives cared for them. Her personal god, Spencer Tracy (few men ever make personal gods out of their women), had his wife, Louise, who devoted her life to caring for their two children, Susan and John. He had Hepburn, who devoted her life to caring for him, and he had various ladies on the side. He took little interest in anyone's welfare, including, it must be said, his own.

While it's true that Hepburn had Phyllis Wilbourn, the devoted secretary/companion she inherited from Constance Collier, the classically trained British actress turned acting coach, and a housekeeper/cook, she was still involved in every aspect of running her household, as well as Tracy's. A woman who supports her husband, who expects him to oversee the domestic sphere, and their children, and who considers her time off from work as free time to work on her golf game, or to put her feet up and get caught up on her favorite television programs—this woman lives like a man. Then, as now, this woman is rare. For Hepburn, "living like a man" meant sacrificing that which men are never asked to sacrifice, in order to do what she damned well pleased.

There was also the curious business with her money. Hepburn—the model of personal independence—sent all her checks to Hep, who managed her finances until his death in 1962. She had to be the only fifty-five-year-old "independent" woman in Christiandom still receiving an allowance from her dad. There are several stories about how this arrangement came about. One story says that when she divorced Luddy, her father discovered she'd spent $100,000 of Luddy's money, and the frugal Hep simply couldn't tolerate his eldest daughter exhibiting spendthrift ways; another says that when she received her first check from RKO, she cashed it, stuck the money in a drawer, and spent every penny. Hep, hearing of this, took command of Kate's finances there and then—her agent and paramour Leland Hayward had been doing them before—and doled out every cent to her from that moment on.

◆–◆–◆

Unlike most of us, Hepburn understood intuitively that the peculiarities of her personality were to be embraced. During her early, contentious years in Hollywood, people assumed that Hepburn never knew the unkind things people said about her, for the simple reason that if she *knew*, she would have made an effort to change. Because she didn't, they assumed she was not only ill-dressed and ill-mannered, but oblivious as well. Really, would it have killed her to don a skirt, hold her tongue, or powder her nose?

The answer is yes, little by little it would have. Contrary to the conventional wisdom put forth today by marketing experts, who've insinuated themselves into every facet of contemporary life, success does not rest on giving people what they want. Perhaps this works in the short run, if you are a snack food (does anyone remember Space Food Sticks or Ice Cream Soda in a can?) or Britney Spears, but for most human beings it's only good advice if you want to chip away at your own true self.

Hepburn knew that the key to success in life and work rested in cultivating her own personality, and that the key to fully and successfully inhabiting your life meant embracing every contradictory quality you owned. As her star rose, she realized she could do anything she pleased as long as she eluded classification. As she got the hang of Hollywood, she realized this meant only taking roles that were—or seemed to be—written for her. If a producer said, "Get me Hepburn!" she determined it would be based on her singularity and not because she played the best damsel in distress, or the best wisecracking career girl, or the best doomed heroine with a terminal disease. She was an early practitioner of self-branding. She was the Brand Called Kate.

To compromise that which she knew to be true about herself, even in the smallest of ways, would be to initiate the erosion of her singularity. Thus, she worked her eccentricities. She embraced the contradictions in her nature. She was happy to be seen as a strange beast.

Several Noted Hepburn Eccentricities, Which She Cultivated

- She was obsessed with flowers. She couldn't relax unless fresh flowers were in every room. When she repaired to Fenwick from her town house in New York, she would take the flowers with her. Sometimes, she could be seen leaping out of the car to pick wildflowers by the side of the road.

- She was equally obsessed with hydration, both drinking enough water and making sure people urinated frequently.

- She didn't like eating out in restaurants because she found them too expensive. She ate fast and became anxious when people watched her eat. Once, in the Cochon d'Or, in Paris, she was so nervous she fainted.

- She kept a fire burning in the fireplace at all times, even in L.A., even in the summer.

- She was conscientious about maintaining her unique "Bryn Mawr" accent. How else to explain the lack of anything approaching a West Coast inflection after decades of living off and on in L.A.?

o She took a gazillion showers every day. She made sure everyone knew about what can only be called a fetish. She also fueled the legend that she refused to rent a house before she tried out the shower, which allegedly also meant leaving the rental agent standing in the foyer, waiting, while Miss Hepburn rinsed off.

o She never sat in a chair if she could help it. Her customary after-dinner position? Sprawled out on her stomach. "Helps the digestion."

o For a time her favorite piece of outerwear was the removable liner of a trench coat that she'd found.

o In later life, after the truth about her relationship with Tracy came out, she was delighted to be known as both an insufferable diva and a devoted and slavish caretaker.

o At seventy-one she took up jogging. With Greta Garbo, then seventy-three.

It's ironic that in the Golden Age of Hollywood, when both society and culture were far more circumscribed, when doing your own proverbial thing, coloring outside the lines, and thinking outside the box were not considered virtues, actresses of Hepburn's stature strove for uniqueness. Garbo was pure mystery with her sloe eyes and deep voice. Bette Davis had that famous mouth, curious diction, and rock-lyric-inspiring eyes. Lauren Bacall was a home-grown exotic, with her honey-colored hair and jungle-cat grace. They all made it their business to be one of a kind, to strive to be in no one else's category but their own.

How different from today. We are all alleged nonconformists, with our individual playlists, our sassy bumper stickers, small-of-the-back tattoos, and pierced parts. I'm always reminded of the great scene from Monty Python's *Life of Brian*. Brian tells his followers, "You've got to think for yourselves. You're all individuals!" And the crowd recites, "Yes, we're all individuals!" And one lone voice in the crowd pipes up in a cockney accent, "I'm not!"

The truth embedded in this squib of Pythonic satire can be seen in the behavior of today's top actresses: the first thing they do upon earning an ounce of fame is go blond and lose weight. More weight, I should say, because they're probably already thin and lovely, hence the fame. Even stars whose remarkable heads of hair are an enormous part of their original appeal don't seem at home in themselves until they've hit the peroxide. They can't ditch their individuality fast enough.

◆—◆

Goldie Hawn once famously said, "There are three ages for women in Hollywood—Babe, District Attorney, and Driving Miss Daisy." Hepburn's career defied categorization, but it did not entirely defy this model.

Her Babe phase saw her playing English girls, as she did in her first two movies, *A Bill of Divorcement* and *Christopher Strong*. In *Morning Glory*, her Eva Lovelace was a babe in the woods, dazzled by the idea of making it on Broadway; she was a Babe with a mission. Jo March is young and vital but she is no Babe. Was dotty heiress Susan Vance in *Bringing Up Baby* a Babe? It's hard to say. She was awfully sexy chasing around that leopard. Linda Seton in *Holiday* was a babe in a gilded cage; she ran off with Johnny Case (Cary Grant) for reasons having to do with freedom as much as love. Hepburn's career-defining Tracy Lord in *The Philadelphia Story* was a goddess who transformed into a Babe and was thus made more accessible. Hepburn's Babes were babes only by virtue of her age. Mostly, the Hepburn heroine was a beauty who gave men a run for their money.

Hepburn's Late Babe phase (dated from roughly 1942 through 1949) was occupied by her movies with Spencer Tracy. Being the female half of a romantic-comedy team is not an option today because the romantic-comedy team no longer exists; there is no equivalent to Tracy and Hepburn today. Meg Ryan and Tom Hanks in *Sleepless in Seattle* (1993) and *You've Got Mail* (1998) are the best we have to offer, and even their movies hail from an era when Hollywood still considered the comedy of romance a viable topic for a big movie. The only couples who still appear locked in the same relational dynamic in film after film are law enforcement officers, X-Men or other superheroes, and of course, the young pubescent wizards Harry and Hermione.

Hepburn's District Attorney stage was, of necessity, the Spinster in Desperate Need of Lovin' stage. In the fifties, there was no other choice. Movies have always reflected the zeitgeist, and Hepburn predates Hawn and her observation by several decades. Even though Kate played an attorney in *Adam's Rib*, the movies of the era weren't yet ready to portray a complex, ambitious, career-driven woman who would also like to be in love. It was inconceivable that if you were a woman over forty, you'd have anything on your mind other than trying to hop on the marriage train before it pulled out of the station for good. After *The African Queen*, Hepburn embraced her old-maid persona. It seems as if every year there was a new movie in which the strong and sturdy Hepburn was perishing for lack of a man's attention.

In *Summertime* (1955), Hepburn stars as the plucky executive secretary Jane Hudson of Akron, Ohio, who takes herself on a trip to Venice. The film is fifty-two years old and shot in somewhat tacky Technicolor, but Venice, as beheld by director David Lean, will never again look so ravishing. Hepburn, who stars opposite the beautiful Rossano Brazzi, looks ruddy and fit and not as if she labors away under fluorescent lights eight hours a day. I sound like my mother, but it's nice to see Hepburn in a dress, and she wears a pair of gorgeous red shoes one fears will get lost during one long night of falling in love. Despite an unintentionally hilarious scene in which the wickedly sexy Brazzi apologizes for failing to be the big steak Hepburn dreams of instead of the ravioli he knows he is, he is the perfect suitor. But he is married, although separated from his signora, and Jane must immediately send herself home, rather than do what Katharine Hepburn would have done—chuck the job in Akron, move to Venice, and take care of Rossano Brazzi.

I won't even go into Hepburn's agitated performance in *The Rainmaker* (1956) as Lizzie Curry, the hysterical spinster whose head is going to explode if she doesn't immediately find someone to marry and enslave herself to. In several fascinating scenes Hepburn mocks men who deplore intelligence in a woman; the character is frustrated by it, but it looks as if Hepburn might actually see the merits in this. Burt Lancaster is Starbuck, the con man with the heart of gold, not to mention an Axis II personality disorder, who lets her in on a secret: once a man—any man—thinks you're beautiful, then you *become* beautiful.

I never saw *The Iron Petticoat*, in which Hepburn plays a Russian aviatrix who defects to the West to play Bob Hope's straight man; I couldn't bear to.

In *Desk Set*, Hepburn's casual, engaging penultimate pairing with Tracy, Hepburn's Bunny Watson is a spry, cheery single gal who's found a family with her fellow single working-gal employees. When Bunny isn't busy running the research department of a large, IBM-like corporation, she's shopping for gowns she can't afford, hoping against hope that Gig Young will ask her to "the dance at the club," and then, perhaps, to marry him!

Mercifully, Hepburn's Spinster in Desperate Need of Lovin' Phase, in which she collaborated in making herself seem woefully asexual and pathetic, lasted only a few years. She was never good at playing average women with modest aspirations, and here she was, now, in middle age, portraying average women at their groveling worst, desperate not to miss out on the only life experience that counted. It's an odd experience watching these movies now, knowing that Hepburn was the diametric opposite of these women. Not only was she unmarried and far from desperate, she had a challenging and interesting career she'd made for herself, money, power, adulation, and the love of a man (to whom she was not married) she respected and adored.

For three good decades no one knew what to make of Hepburn. She was both tomboyish and elegant; she ran around in those baggy pants held together with safety pins, but looked fabulous in high fashion; she was outspoken, yet desperately private, even shy; she was puritanical in her daily habits, yet freethinking when it came to love. Even in the fifties, when the plush, oversized, oversexed Marilyn Monroe was trying to figure out how to marry a millionaire, the skinny-girl jock Hepburn jogged beside Tracy in *Pat and Mike*, in her gray sweatpants, unconcerned about the new role of cleavage in the Hollywood movie. The famous Hepburn made it her job to traffic in contradiction.

Then a strange thing happened in the 1960s: she who had spent a lifetime working to stay out of step with the world, now found that being out of step with the world was in style. It became chic to defy categorization. The times had finally caught up with her. Only a few blocks away from the town house she owned on East Forty-ninth Street in the Turtle Bay neighborhood of Manhattan, *Hair: The American Tribal Love-Rock Musical,* was selling out nightly on Broadway. Over on Park Avenue, Leonard Bernstein was throwing a party for the Black Panthers.

Still, the times were no match for Hepburn, the Master Contrarian.

AREAS IN WHICH HEPBURN REFUSED TO GO ALONG

Feminism

Hepburn was not a feminist. She was a Hepburnist. She believed in the cause of Katharine Hepburn, and in that this cause shared anything with the ideals of feminism, she was all for it. (Question: why does the term *women's lib* elicit guffaws of irony and eye-rolling, when the term *affirmative action*, which entered the vernacular at the same time, does not?)

When questioned about it, as she frequently was, she was dismissive. She claimed not to know what all the fuss was about, that women had done "all that" years ago. The "all that" to which she referred was the suffragette movement and the fight for birth-control rights, the twin battles that consumed her mother, Kit, and her cowarriors Margaret Sanger and Emmeline Pankhurst. Surely Hepburn was being disingenuous, attempting to play off her refusal to become the poster girl for the movement. Or perhaps growing up Hepburn was similar to growing up in a family of football players or classical musicians; as an adult you never quite believe the entire world doesn't share your family's obsession. Her family was so progressive, with women's rights in the very air at her childhood home in Hartford, she might well not have known what all the fuss was about, and why hordes of women were claiming her as their idol. It's doubtful; Hepburn didn't miss much. As Nietzche said, "The thinking man is not a party man," and Katharine Hepburn was never a party woman.

Hepburn always made a point of championing the work of wives and mothers, but she spoke about it as if the whole thing really had nothing to do with her, the way people living in a country at peace talk about the courage of the citizens in a war-torn land. "Being a housewife and a mother is the biggest job in the world, but if it doesn't interest you, don't do it—I would have made a terrible mother" was her characteristic dismissal of a question most of us lose plenty of sleep over.

Hepburn was equally firm in her belief that a woman couldn't combine a career and children. You had to pick one or the other. You could not possibly be the mother of one and work part-time. You couldn't have three children and a husband who worked at home. She was inflexible on this point (perhaps because to entertain alternatives might have led her to question her own decisions, and Kate was not a believer in entertaining doubt, ever). Women, who, she did allow, were more complex and interesting than men, simply had to make the choice and live with it. "I've had a fascinating life," she said, "but I haven't had everything."

The Counterculture

Hepburn's attitude surrounding the making of *Guess Who's Coming to Dinner* in 1967 is an indication of the degree to which Hepburn gave two hoots about the state of the world during the most turbulent decade of the century. Stanley Kramer, along with screenwriter William Rose, had hatched a story about a girl bringing home her fiancé for her parents to meet. The man was a brilliant doctor, also wealthy, cultured, and kind. The catch is that he's Sidney Poitier. This was the first major Hollywood movie to take interracial marriage as its subject, and Hepburn sat in her customary place at Tracy's feet as Kramer pitched him the idea. Hepburn couldn't have cared less about the precedent she and Tracy were about to set. When the film went into production, interracial marriage was still illegal in seventeen states. Would *Guess Who's Coming to Dinner* make a difference? Create a stir? Attract picketers? The only thing she cared about was getting Tracy back to work again. His health was so bad he was uninsurable, and both Hepburn and Kramer gambled on him by putting their own salaries in an account that would cover reshoots with another actor should Tracy be unable to finish.

The film was a legendary success—the biggest hit either Tracy, Hepburn, or Tracy/Hepburn ever made, making a boatload of money for Columbia and winning Hepburn her second Best Actress Oscar. Hepburn was instantly "relevant." Tracy, because he was the dubious, stodgy father who needed to be convinced that his little girl was safe with Sidney Poitier, and because he looked

old and ill (he died two weeks after shooting was finished), did not
gain the same countercultural cred.

But Hepburn was not intrigued. In her increasingly frequent
interviews she claimed to be apolitical. This was the same person
who had jeopardized her young career decades earlier by support-
ing the socialist Upton Sinclair for governor of California and
worn a red dress to give a public endorsement of progressive pres-
idential candidate Henry A. Wallace, just as Hollywood was being
eyed as a possible communist stronghold by Joseph McCarthy.

Hepburn had nothing to say about the Vietnam War. She was
against drug-taking in any form and couldn't see why no one liked
Richard Nixon.

Movies
If there was one place where Hepburn's censorious, schoolmarmish
nature could be glimpsed in full, it was in her feelings toward the
groundbreaking movies of the late sixties and early seventies. She
snorted at movies like the critically acclaimed 1969 *Midnight Cowboy,* starring Jon Voight and Dustin Hoffman as a pair of street hus-
tlers (Voight's Joe Buck hustled rich society women; Hoffman's
sickly Ratso Rizzo hustled Joe Buck), believing a movie needed a
proper hero and heroine. She was firmly against antiheroes and
-heroines of every stripe. Despite her own androgyny, men needed
to be men and women needed to be women. She sniffed at movies
that took as their subject people's sexual awakenings, which she
called "a bo-aah," in her inimitable accent.

She dismissed an entire decade and a half of revolutionary

filmmaking in *Me: Stories of My Life*: "John Wayne is the hero of the thirties and forties and most of the fifties. Before the creeps came creeping in. Before . . . the male hero slid right down into the valley of the weak and the misunderstood. Before women began dropping any pretense to virginity in the gutter. With a disregard for truth which is indeed pathetic."

One isn't quite sure what she's getting at here, but her rather quotidian opinion is clear: they sure didn't make movies like they used to.

Free Love
As you might imagine, Hepburn found it completely appalling.

3

THE NECESSITY OF HAVING AN
AVIATOR IN YOUR LIFE

Early Hollywood and the Question of What to Do with the Likes of Hepburn;
Making Movies Is Not for the Faint of Heart; Kate's Capacity for Friendships;
Types of Friends Worth Having and Keeping; An Aviator Is Good for the Soul

The early days of Hepburn's career coincided with the early
days of the Golden Age of Hollywood—defined as *The Jazz
Singer* (1927) through, let's say, *Adam's Rib* (1949)—when movies
tumbled out of the studios and into theaters like Wonka Bars off
the end of Willy's conveyor belts. The five big studios were cities
unto themselves, each with its own police department, post office,
and lock shop. They employed an eager army of producers, directors, screenwriters, art directors, costume designers, editors, and
soundmen to churn out westerns, screwball comedies, musicals,
and costume dramas, never realizing they were making movies
that would one day be considered classics. The studios owned the
theaters, and the theaters needed movies, so out came stuff that
was genius, insufferable tripe, or somewhere in between.

Movies weren't considered art, so there was little anguish. Film production zipped right along. It was unheard of for a script to go through twenty-seven drafts, as is common today, or for a persnickety director to wait until the perfect A-list actor was out of rehab to begin shooting. Movies were all shot on huge, windowless soundstages, or on studio back lots, their Wild West or turn-of-the-century English streets baking beneath the reliably pale, cloud-free California skies.

After Hepburn caught the nation's attention in *A Bill of Divorcement*, RKO put her under contract, and voilà, a few short months later she starred in *Christopher Strong*, in which she played Lady Cynthia Darrington, a famous unmarried aviatrix who finds herself pregnant by a married member of Parliament (the eponymous Christopher Strong). Of course, Lady Cynthia had no choice but to commit suicide at thirty thousand feet by removing her oxygen mask and plummeting dramatically to her death.

Although no one knew it then, this was the beginning of Hepburn's lifelong cinematic troubles. She was born to play women several decades ahead of their time who were coolly sexy and sassy, with defined deltoids and a golf-course stride, who lived life on their own terms; fine, as far as it goes, but what could, in the end, possibly become of such a person? In *Christopher Strong*, it was inconceivable that Lady Darrington would complete her successful circumnavigation of the globe, handily give birth as a single mother, taking her child out in a blue pram every morning for a nice airing, or that she would press Christopher Strong to divorce Lady Strong. As would be the case for almost all of Hepburn's independent women, there were two options: kill them off or marry them off. Death being the universal downer that it is, Hepburn more often than not found herself disingenuously collapsing into a puddle of misty-eyed love for her oft-times inferior leading man in the last reel of every movie.

Only fifteen months separated *A Bill of Divorcement* from *Morning Glory*, for which Hepburn won her first Best Actress Oscar. She played the chatty, naïve-to-the-point-of-mildly-deranged aspiring actress Ada Love, who changes her name to Eva Lovelace. ("It's partly made up and partly real. It was Ada Love. Love's my family name. I added the *lace*. Do you like it, or would you prefer something shorter? A shorter name would be more convenient on a sign. Still, 'Eva Lovelace in *Camille*,' for instance, or 'Eva Lovelace in *Romeo and Juliet*' sounds very distinguished, doesn't it?")

Despite the Oscar, RKO hadn't yet figured out what to do with Hepburn (and despite her self-possession, Hepburn hadn't yet figured out what to do with herself). Cranky British portrait photographer and costume designer Cecil Beaton, who would cross paths with Hepburn decades down the road during the Broadway run of *Coco* and despise her ("She is the egomaniac of all time"), still acknowledged she had a face made for the camera.

In those early films Hepburn is as strange-looking as she is incandescent. Had she been born decades later, she could easily have been cast as an Elvin queen in one of the overblown fantasy epics we're so fond of these days. In every close-up her puckish androgyny collides head-on with her luminous charisma. *Morning*

Glory is nearly seventy-five years old, and you can see her fresh appeal still. The clean lines of her clothes straddled the border between elegant and plain. Despite whatever beauty and charm her female costars possessed, they looked overdone. The adage about looking chic that advises glancing in the mirror before you go out and removing one accessory, apparently never reached their ears. They wore aggressive hats that made them look like exotic birds, dresses with curiously fussy necklines, and oddly designed wraps that were undoubtedly the height of fashion. Their hair was adamantly set and coiffed. Beside Hepburn, with her short bob that always looked as if she'd just dashed in from somewhere, they looked like matrons or men in drag.

RKO was flummoxed. Hepburn was too contemporary for comfort. They tried to diffuse her odd appeal by sticking her in period pieces set in England. They put her in strange costumes and doomed her to a series of unlikely professions and love affairs that even in other times and other places would never have transpired.

After *Little Women*, in which George Cukor, directing her for the second time, employed Hepburn's tomboy brashness to excellent effect as Jo March, she dutifully starred in two stinkeroos a year, with the exception of 1936, in which she starred in three. She played Trigger, the illiterate Ozark Mountains faith healer, and Babbie, a wild gypsy who liked to sing and incite laborers to riot. She played an aspiring composer named rather pretentiously Constance Dane Roberti, who endures a drunken folie à deux with a philandering conductor. She played Mary Stuart, Queen of

Scotland, who returned to England only to have her head lopped off by her smarter, craftier sister, Elizabeth I.

In her most infamous flop, Hepburn played Sylvia Scarlett, the daughter of Henry Scarlett, an English embezzler living in France who must escape to England. Sylvia becomes Sylvester to avoid detection. Hepburn looked so handsome as a young man, the moviegoers of the nation ran screaming. The gender-bending, though utterly harmless, was too much.

◆—◆

Even though most of Hepburn's films from these years missed, she remained undaunted. Her work ethic was legendary. She gained a reputation as the most punctual actor in Hollywood. She arrived on the set at six A.M. and left at six P.M., six days a week. On Sunday, she played tennis, golfed. Somewhere in there, she also made time to take her legendary handful of showers, have a swim, and make the acquaintance of dozens of people who became friends for life. They don't make movies like they used to, nor do people make friends like they used to.

As Robert Putnam noted in his insightful and somewhat depressing book *Bowling Alone: The Collapse and Revival of American Community*, adults aren't much interested in making friends anymore. Across the board, we're less interested in our acquaintances from church, our second cousins, and the neighbor two houses down we always run into when we're out walking the dog. Research shows that the positive effects of friendship are comparable to being on a good antidepressant, and that the more friends a person has, the less sick she's likely to be; still, we're all too busy, and it's too much effort. When we do have a few spare hours, we'd rather surf the Web, or, yes, bowl alone.

No one who works twelve hours a day, six days a week, as did Hepburn, also joins the PTA, plans a block party, hosts a weekly bridge party, or volunteers. We don't tell people to drop by whenever. We don't tell them to call us if they need a ride to or from the airport. The cocktail party is dead and so is the Sunday brunch and sending out Christmas cards. College students have friends, it's true; they hang out and hook up, activities that rarely involve changing clothes or leaving the sofa. The only people who can afford the luxury of having friends are teenagers, or adults living in the *Seinfeld*-ian mode of arrested development.

Hepburn found the time to make and sustain friendships in part because despite her much vaunted independence, she hated to be alone. Like so many people born before the age of the microchip, Hepburn was a frantic and avid writer of letters. She sat in bed in the morning and dashed off reams of them or hastily scribbled them on the back of script pages during the day's filming and sent them off without a thought.

Hepburn was a freewheeling, confident collector of people whom she found intriguing, a person who apparently had no trouble sniffing out bootlickers, brownnosers, and toadies of all stripes. In her Living Legend years a few more sycophants found their way into her living room than when she was just starting out, but mostly the people who got close to Hepburn became true friends and, over the decades, remained true friends. Even Hepburn's ex-husband, Luddy, remained her friend until his death at age eighty, and her ex-boyfriends (or whatever we're to call the men she involved herself with pre-Tracy) could be counted on for companionship and favors until they, too, expired.

If you were Hepburn's friend, you could count on her to go to dramatic lengths for you. Perhaps this is how true friendships were conducted then. If someone was your friend, it was understood that he or she would consume your time, inconvenience you, fail to respect your "boundaries" (which in those times were associated with maps, field sports, borders between nations, and had nothing to do with people), and in general make demands. Hepburn, if she was your friend, could be counted on to feed you innumerable meals, help you nurse a hangover (she was good at this, on account of her time in the trenches with Spencer Tracy), or bring you some of her special lace cookies when you were sick.

People who study such things have discovered that women tend to conduct their friendships face-to-face and men conduct their friendships side by side. Hepburn preferred the side-by-side method. She preferred someone who would stand her nine holes to a coffee klatch any day. Her solution to any insoluble problem a friend might timidly wish to discuss would always be to either jump into a cold shower or take up watercolors. Brooding of any kind was not something in which she was interested, for herself or anyone else.

To be Hepburn's friend could be like galloping a willful horse uphill. You had to cope with her compulsive bossiness, her well-meaning determination to offer heaps of unsolicited advice. You had to put up with her astonishing energy, her love of gossip but disinclination to go out and collect it herself (she was famously adverse to partygoing), her devotion to sport, work, rising at the same predawn hour as dairy farmers. You were also expected to agree with her; and since she had definite opinions about most everything, this could be the most taxing aspect of all. During the filming of *Without Love* in 1944, producer Lawrence Weingarten is said to have said, "Even looking at pictures of Katharine Hepburn makes me tired."

As Garson Kanin, one of Hepburn's lifelong friends and the screenwriter of *Adam's Rib* and *Pat and Mike*, writes in *Tracy and Hepburn: An Intimate Memoir* (Hepburn pitched a fit when the book was published, but later grew to approve of the way she and Tracy were portrayed), "Kate knows a lot about a lot and is only too eager, at any time, to pass it on. Where to live and how. Which side of the street is great, which side is hopeless. Exactly where in the bedroom the bed should be placed. How to refrigerate food. What to put on a chigger bite. What to feed a dog. Dentistry. How to keep water out of your ears when swimming. Literature. Weather. The tides. How to drive a car in the city, the country, on the road. Birth. Death. Mortality. How to age gracefully."

You could also glimpse Hepburn's capacity for friendship and connection in her movies. Hepburn was not a versatile actor, but she was a master at imbuing her characters with recognizable aspects of her own personality. Even in movies and plays where she was determinedly Not Hepburn—all those mad mothers and widows she played in late middle age, the predatory Violet Venable in

Tennessee Williams's *Suddenly, Last Summer*, the fragile, depressed Mary Tyrone in Eugene O'Neill's *Long Day's Journey into Night*—the audience always had a sense that she was playing a personally familiar chord.

In *Little Women* we can see Hepburn's domineering tomboy Jo befriend her sisters, lavishing adoration and orders upon them in equal measure; she roughhouses with and helps shore up Laurie, the rich boy next door who eventually falls in love with her. In *Stage Door*, even though Hepburn's rich girl Terry Randall is shunned by the other residents of the Footlights Club, the all-female boarding-house that caters to aspiring actresses suffering from the drama bug, she pines to be part of the crowd, lending Ginger Rogers's Jean Maitland a fur coat for an upcoming date and attempting to partic-ipate in all the wisecracking.

Even though *Desk Set* purported to offer audiences another cocktail of Tracy-Hepburn chemistry, the real effervescence oc-curs between Hepburn's Bunny Watson and her coworkers, Peg (Joan Blondell), Sylvia (Dina Merrill), and Ruthie (Sue Randall). The girls throw an office Christmas party—complete with extra-fizzy champagne that drenches all the paperwork, and an upright piano on casters they roll from office to office, complete with drunken piano player—that looks like so much fun it could single-handedly revamp the entire dreaded institution. Collectively, they worry about their jobs, their futures, and their men, but no situa-tion seems too dire as long as they have each other.

◆—◆

It stands to reason that if we are no longer keen on seeking out friends and cultivating friendships, we also no longer possess different kinds of friends. The lucky, sociable ones among us may have one good friend from college, one good friend we made as an adult, and a spouse or spouse-equivalent. We know people from work and from the gym, and we may be on a first-name basis with the parents of the children who play soccer with our kids. Otherwise, the pickings are slim.

Friends have gone the way of hats. Do you own a single hat, aside from a baseball cap you might throw on to walk in the rain? During the era in which Hepburn became a star, women possessed entire hat wardrobes. They owned different hats for churchgoing, for attending luncheons and parties, for weddings and funerals. They owned perky hats meant to be worn at a tilt; high-crowned hats that made them look imperious; flat, wide sailorlike hats, turbans, and snoods. A new hat was guaranteed to cheer a girl right up, and no one complained of hat hair, so beloved were hats. The only places people wear hats now are costume parties and the Kentucky Derby.

Hat wardrobes are unlikely ever to make a serious comeback, but I'm simply unwilling to believe the same is true of human friendship. Perhaps inspiration can be found not only in the breadth of Hepburn's friendships, but also in their depth and variety.

The Laura Harding Friend
The Laura Harding Friend is the sidekick friend (if she is also your lesbian lover, that's your business). If, like Hepburn, you have no

real use for buddies who are your equals, the sidekick friend is right up your alley. The sidekick is the friend who goes along with all of your ideas, even if an idea is terrible, requires some convincing on your part, and may ultimately require the services of a good lawyer. Every once in a while you give in and placate the sidekick by letting her call the shots; this is done mostly to show that you're not a dictatorial monster, but a decent soul worthy of having a sidekick. It's understood that whenever you go anywhere with your sidekick, it is the sidekick who is accompanying *you*, and not the other way around. Despite the seeming inequity of the situation, a sidekick is a genuine friend; she is not a hanger-on. You love your sidekick; in some cases you wouldn't be you without her.

The sidekick for whom Hepburn was most famous was Laura Harding, always described as "the American Express heiress." Few of Harding's millions actually came from American Express, but it's a handy way to signify that this girl had money. Her father was a financier. She grew up in a stone mansion on Fifth Avenue. At the time she met Hepburn in New York, when both girls were aspiring actresses studying with voice coach Frances Robinson-Duff, Laura Harding was worth $7 million, or roughly $80 million in 2006 dollars.

Next to Hepburn, with her architectural bone structure, voice that sounded like a child's sled dragged over a gravel road, self-described country-bumpkin sense of style, and brash behavior, Harding was pretty and saucy, but otherwise unremarkable. She was not considered "an original," "a character," or "a personage," as was her friend Kathy. Harding was debutante-sleek and well-modulated, an aimless rich girl down to her DNA, and thus available to drop everything at a moment's notice and accompany Hepburn to Hollywood. Upon setting up housekeeping in their sprawling Coldwater Canyon ranch house, Kate and Laura set about becoming the prototypes for Lucy and Ethel.

Hepburn liked people who were capable of playing pranks and practical jokes. She and Laura Harding enjoyed many glamorous Hollywood parties; they rarely attended, but preferred to amuse themselves by breaking into the empty houses of the people who did. Apocryphal stories have the girls crashing one party dressed as the kitchen help and sneaking into a famous producer's house hidden in the trunk of a car. When they were not breaking and entering, or tooling around town acting as if they were better than everyone else, Hepburn was at work, and Harding was either shopping for antiques on behalf of their new friend George Cukor (see below), or bringing Hepburn lunch, or, most important, behaving in the heiresslike manner Kate would make her own.

During the filming of *A Bill of Divorcement* Harding was a fixture on the set. She was eventually offered $10 to play an extra in the opening party scene. Hepburn, in her first star entrance, soars down a curving staircase and straight into the arms of her handsome fiancé (David Manners). Harding wanders down in the background, to join her own beau in a dance. During shooting, when Harding reached the bottom of the stair, the newel post came off in her hand. Confused by this prop malfunction, she laughed and handed the newel to the extra playing her boyfriend, who shrieked with surprise and outrage. Harding couldn't contain herself. Like Kit and Hep, who felt their daughter was devoting her life to something superficial and ridiculous, Harding had a tough time taking the movies seriously. Cukor marched over and gave Harding a good slap for her amateurism.

It should be noted that this was not simply because she was a known sidekick; the great women's director Cukor also smacked Hepburn during the filming of *Little Women* when she was messing around and dropped ice cream on the only dress they'd made for a particular scene.

Laura Harding may have been Hepburn's most well-known sidekick, but she was not the first. That honor belongs to Bryn Mawr classmate Alice Palache, plain-featured and whip smart, who helped Hepburn raise her failing grades. The summer before their senior year they drove round Britain in a used car. Or rather Palache did. Hepburn decided she was born to be the passenger and documentarian of their journey. While Palache drove—she was always Palache, never Alice—Hepburn wrote poetry about the mean accommodations and frightening toilets they stumbled upon. Palache also handled their money, something she would do again for her enormously famous friend many years later when Palache was senior vice president at the Fiduciary Trust Company. In true sidekick fashion she undertook the chore of managing her old friend's finances without complaint.

Irene Selznick was the sidekick of Hepburn's middle age. In the early fifties Hepburn lived with Selznick on Summit Drive in Beverly Hills. They amused themselves by sneaking into the swimming pools of friends.

Selznick was no star, but as the daughter of Louis B. Mayer, the onetime wife of David O. Selznick, and the producer of a little play called *A Streetcar Named Desire*, her theatrical pedigree was impeccable. She was brilliant in her own right—not ideal sidekick material—but by the time she and Hepburn vacationed in Jamaica with Noël Coward in 1953, Hepburn had just starred in *The African Queen*, which solidified her gargantuan fame once and for all. Anyone who became acquainted with Hepburn after this was perforce destined to be a sidekick.

The Phelpie Friend

I won't lie to you: the Phelpie Friend is rare. Most of us go through our entire lives never enjoying even a passing friendship with one. The Phelpie Friend is named after the now nearly forgotten poet H. Phelps Putman (his legacy suffered in part because however you scrambled his name, it sounds correct. Is he Phelps H. Putman? Putman H. Phelps?), who was a darkly handsome tortured genius, fond of booze, sex, his roguish reputation, long-winded ruminations on the nature of God, and a certain Miss Hepburn. Phelpie was married. He was tortured. Wait, I just said that. Edmund Wilson praised his debut volume of verse, published when Phelpie was just thirty-three, as one of the best books of poetry in the English language. After that accolade, it was impossible for poor Phelpie to write another word.

It was the era of the speakeasy. Phelpie would leave his long-suffering wife, Ruth, in their claustrophobic apartment on the top floor of his parents' house in a dreary Boston suburb and make his way to Greenwich Village, to hook up with the likes of Robert

Benchley, Dorothy Parker, and young Kate, his professed muse, who enchanted them all with her weird wardrobe, compulsive ladies' room visiting (the result of her dutiful water consuming, as advised by her urologist father), and noisy slurping of cheap whiskey from chipped coffee cups. Phelpie orchestrated their collective awe at her originality.

Phelpie's worship of Hepburn was unabashed, melodramatic. He was bowled over at the mere existence of her. He marveled at her body, which he compared to a dagger. He referred to her as "his nourishment." He dedicated his next major poem to her, "The Daughters of the Sun." In our time, there are few poets of any stature, and I hazard to say none at all that trade in being tortured romantics. Are there even any muses left?

The Cukor Friend

Named for the incomparable and underappreciated George Cukor, director of such stylish Hollywood classics as *Dinner at Eight*, *The Women*, *Born Yesterday*, *It Should Happen to You*, *My Fair Lady*, and, at age eighty-two, *Rich and Famous*, starring Candice Bergen and Jacqueline Bisset (his old friend Katharine Hepburn thought the movie all right, but there was too much sex in it). The Cukor Friend is the comrade-in-arms, the friend with whom you share a lifelong passion. Perhaps you make the acquaintance of the Cukor Friend in a college art history class, or on a softball team. It's not unheard of for the Cukor Friend to become a business partner. Great adventures are embarked upon with The Cukor Friend.

Perhaps because Cukor's movies routinely featured women

with interior lives and complex personalities, he earned the dubious label "women's director," thus guaranteeing he would never join the ranks of the greats. It matters not that Cukor discovered that Cary Grant was a natural comedian or also pulled Oscar-nomination-worthy performances out of Spencer Tracy, Aldo Ray, James Mason, and Jack Lemmon.

George Cukor did Hepburn the invaluable service of igniting her passion for moviemaking. He was the friend who helped the neophyte actress excel. Anyone who plays tennis knows that the only way you can improve your game is to play with someone better than you, and Hepburn played with Cukor. He directed Hepburn in her comeback vehicle and signature film, *The Philadelphia Story*, and gave the fidgety, high-strung actress an invaluable bit of directorial advice: "Don't just do something, stand there."

The French thought Cukor was a genius, and so did Andy Warhol. Cukor threw tremendous parties every Sunday at his estate high above Sunset Boulevard and helped Hepburn wrangle the increasingly difficult Spencer Tracy in his dotage. Cukor means sugar in Hungarian, and one cannot imagine having a sweeter friend.

Cukor once said, "My chief claim to fame will be that I once lost seventy-two pounds and I fired Bette Davis." Of course, his other claim to fame was that he contributed to the invention of Katharine Hepburn.

The Hayward-Hughes Friend

During a time in which people crossed the country by train and the ocean by ship, Hepburn had not one but two aviators in her

life: her agent, Leland Hayward, and infamous millionaire kook
Howard Hughes.

Hayward was there for Hepburn from the day she arrived in
Hollywood. He was a forerunner of the glamorous Hollywood
power agent. Even in 1932 he spent all his time on the phone. He
kept a fabulous tailored wardrobe, possessed many pairs of fine
shoes. He was a dandy who liked to flirt and couldn't care less
about sports, married not once but twice to a woman named Lola
Gibbs, who caused him no small amount of anguish. For a time,
he shacked up with Hepburn and Laura Harding in their rented
Coldwater Canyon ranch house. Hayward conferred upon the
quiet household Hollywood glamour and Hollywood gossip. He
and Kate had a desultory something or other.

In recent times there's been a lot of talk that Hayward was
simply Hepburn's beard, and maybe he was. The press loved con-
juring up torrid love affairs for Hepburn, and the nation always
liked her much better when she was on the verge of matrimony, so
why not? In any case, it was fun, and Hepburn was all for fun. The
occasional talk of marriage pushed Hepburn into finalizing her divorce from Luddy, who kept hoping she would call for him or
would return East.

Regardless of what was going on between Laura Harding and
Hepburn, nothing was ever going to happen between Hayward
and Hepburn. Hayward lacked the necessary weltschmerz to ever
interest Hepburn romantically, or, to put it another way, he failed
to be a specific sort of impossible, drunken Irishman.

As is true of all friends of the Hayward-Hughes persuasion,

however, Leland was good for some adrenaline-producing adventure (this is the main function of the Hayward-Hughes Friend). Hayward's plane was called *Thunderbird*, and he flew it over the country, from Burbank to Newark and back again, with Hepburn beside him in the cockpit. They would fly all night.

Hepburn's attraction to Howard Hughes was not dissimilar. She loved his compulsive risk-taking, his need to swim upstream, to think big, his refusal to allow himself to be categorized. In that she enjoyed his vast wealth, it was because it allowed him unlimited freedom. The Hayward-Hughes Friend is the wild man who has the money and the means, or the creativity and the fearlessness, the person who shows you the fantastic possibilities.

Hepburn met the rangy, cowboy-bad-guy-looking Howard Hughes when he landed his plane on a beach north of Malibu during the filming of *Sylvia Scarlett*, in 1935. For several years in the late thirties, Hughes and Hepburn were an item, but mostly they enjoyed being notorious together, flying around the country, engaging in lavish hide-and-seek games with desperate reporters and even more desperate photographers, tossing out false engagement rumors, sneaking onto golf courses for a quick nine.

Hughes was routinely trying to break various world air-speed records. He was also a film producer, spending his own millions to make the first blockbuster, *Hell's Angels*. His most famous film was *The Outlaw*, starring the impossible brick house Jane Russell, for whom Hughes had his aircraft engineers design a special cantilevered contraption designed to display her assets; it was a forerunner of the modern push-up bra.

Hepburn loved the romance of her Hughes days, but she could never love Hughes. Setting aside that Hayward-Hughes Friends always make terrible partners (they tend to be bewitched by their own personalities, philander, have odd habits, are possessed by incomprehensible demons, refuse to pick up their socks), Hughes, like Hayward, was peculiar, but not nearly difficult enough to interest Kate.

When it seemed as if there were nothing left for Hughes and Hepburn to do but marry, the relationship died, like a tropical storm that peters out the moment it makes landfall. Hughes did, however, do Hepburn one of the greatest favors of her career: for her birthday he purchased the screen rights to *The Philadelphia Story*.

What is the equivalent of an aviator in these modern times? An arctic explorer? A summiter of Everest? One of those towheaded men who live in cutoffs and traverse the globe in search of the biggest wave? These occupations don't quite capture the proper feeling of both sophistication and freedom inspired by the true Hayward-Hughes Friend. Sir Richard Branson, founder of Virgin Atlantic Airways, comes to mind, but he seems more cagey entrepreneur than blue-sky adventurer. Maybe, at the end of the day, only an old-fashioned aviator will do.

4

HOW TO STICK TO YOUR KNITTING*

1938; Who is Harry Brandt and Why Is He Saying Those Things About Me?; The Poisonous Katharine of Arrogance Will Not Play Scarlett O'Hara; What People Hated About Hepburn; The Importance of Work; Some Hard Truths; Going On When There Seems No Reason to Go On

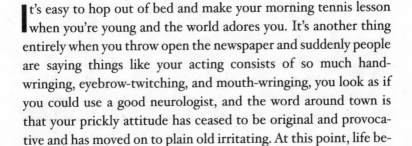

I t's easy to hop out of bed and make your morning tennis lesson when you're young and the world adores you. It's another thing entirely when you throw open the newspaper and suddenly people are saying things like your acting consists of so much hand-wringing, eyebrow-twitching, and mouth-wringing, you look as if you could use a good neurologist, and the word around town is that your prickly attitude has ceased to be original and provocative and has moved on to plain old irritating. At this point, life begins to look a little different.

It was 1938. FDR was in the White House and Benny Goodman

---

*Hepburn actually was a knitter. She favored the English method, also known as the throw method.

was the first jazz musician to headline at Carnegie Hall. Oil was discovered in Saudi Arabia. The first nylon-bristle toothbrush hit the market, as did the first Superman comic. The Spanish Civil War raged on; Franco's government was recognized by the Vatican. *Time*'s Man of the Year was Adolf Hitler, for his convincing "swagger of a conqueror." (As the magazine explained, "On the American scene, 1938 was no one man's year.")

In Hepburn's life, it was the year her desultory suitor Howard Hughes circumnavigated the globe in a world-record-setting ninety-one hours, the year they pretty much realized they would never marry, and the year her childhood vacation home, Fenwick, was destroyed in a hurricane that remains one of the most spectacular natural disasters in American history. Six hundred people were killed during the first hours of the storm. Radio towers were twisted by the wind to resemble discarded candy wrappers, and in Stonington, Connecticut, the entire top floor of a fifty-thousand-square-foot brick factory blew away.

The morning the hurricane hit, Hepburn took her daily swim at eight A.M. She then played nine holes with her friend Red Hammond, made a hole in one on the par-three ninth, and a few hours before the storm made landfall, played in the waves. When the car in which Hammond had driven to Fenwick hurled past them, and the laundry wing at the back of the house sheared off, they grew concerned. That night, after Fenwick sailed off its foundation and out toward sea, Hepburn dug out eighty-five pieces of her mother's silver, as well as her tea service.

In her autobiography Hepburn called the hurricane a great

adventure. Another person more attuned to the cruel metaphors of life might have viewed the storm as emblematic of the calamitous state of her career or would mourn the devastation as the passing, once and for all, of her childhood. Not Hepburn, whose disinclination to think deeply about anything was her great strength and her great, maddening weakness.

In 1938 *Bringing Up Baby* was also released. The titular Baby is a pet leopard owned by daffy heiress Susan Vance (Hepburn). Cary Grant plays David Huxley, a nutty-professor-type paleontologist awaiting the arrival of a rare brontosaurus bone for the completion of a skeleton he's been piecing together for years. Asta—the terrier from *The Thin Man*—plays George, who steals the brontosaurus bone and buries it. Baby escapes. Wacky escapades ensue. Cary Grant makes a memorable appearance in a frilly peignoir. It's the first time Hepburn starred in a comedy, and she turns out to be genuinely funny.

Still, the movie flopped.* The Great Depression had settled in like a bad head cold. No one was interested in the ridiculous adventures of the leopard-owning rich. Director Howard Hawks (the brilliant, the talented) was fired from RKO, and Hepburn resorted yet again to buying herself out of the last of her contract.

Just as Hawks was putting the finishing touches on *Baby*, a nobody named Harry Brandt—well, all right, he was the president of

---

Bringing Up Baby, and Hepburn, have been vindicated by history. Decades later film lovers the world over rediscovered it. *Entertainment Weekly* voted it number twenty-four on its list of greatest films. *Baby* is now considered the best film Howard Hawks ever directed and still generates income for the Hepburn estate.

something called the Independent Theater Owners of America—altered the course of American cinema by publishing his infamous box-office-poison list. Brandt's main gripe was the dull and awful movies being offered theater owners around that time, but the term *box office poison* was simply too delicious; it stuck like caramel sauce to the actors who starred in the movies Brandt cited. Hepburn wasn't alone; other stars slimed with the Brandt-poison included Joan Crawford, Mae West, and Fred Astaire, great talents whose movies were also tanking at the time.

Finally, in the bad year of 1938, Hepburn was resolutely *not* being cast as Scarlett O'Hara in *Gone With the Wind*. Producer David O. Selznick had launched a nationwide search for the perfect Scarlett. All the people who were home and not out at their local movie house watching Hepburn were busy writing letters to David O. Selznick suggesting he screen-test their nieces. Every girl below the Mason-Dixon Line and between the ages of fifteen and thirty-five hoped to be discovered. Every college was scoured. Every little theater group investigated. Stock companies, ditto. The searching for Scarlett went on for two solid years.

The jury is split over whether failing to win the part of Scarlett O'Hara broke Hepburn's nail-tough heart, or whether she couldn't have cared less. Some say Kate knew she wasn't right for the part, but offered to take the role if Selznick couldn't find anyone else; and others say the opposite, that she felt the part was practically written for her and couldn't understand why the producer was wasting so much time and money casting about for some nobody.

Either way, Kate was a competitor; part of her would want to be offered the part, no matter her suitability. But Hepburn was never going to be cast as Scarlett for the simple reason that David O. Selznick, not a big fan of Hepburn's curious charisma, believed that Rhett Butler would have never chased someone like Katharine Hepburn around the block, much less endlessly, passionately, desperately, for all those sad years.

"Hepburn has two strikes against her," Selznick wrote in a memo. "First, the unquestionable and very widespread intense public dislike of her at the moment, and second, the fact that she has yet to demonstrate the sex qualities that are probably the most important of all the many requisites of Scarlett."

◆—◆

Hepburn's star had been on the wane for several years before the box-office-poison pronouncement put her in danger of becoming one of those young actresses who create a flurry of excitement before retiring young to breed dogs or open a restaurant in the Florida Keys.

The year before, Hepburn had costarred—*costarred!*—with Ginger Rogers in *Stage Door.* The studio was hedging its bets. People loved Ginger Rogers. She was perky and agreeable. She did not possess fearsome cheekbones, a bad attitude, or a stuck-up way of talking. She was a kicky, fun-loving gal impossible not to like.

At the time she was also in the midst of reinventing the Hollywood musical with Fred Astaire (about their successful partnership Hepburn said, "She gives him sex; he gives her class"). Audiences loved Rogers's flowing gowns, and the way she made it look as if dancing with Fred Astaire were the best time to be had on earth. She was a Nice Girl. Even though Hepburn won good reviews in *Stage Door* as Terry Randall, the snooty girl brought low, it wasn't enough to halt the avalanche of public loathing.

Like a plane crash, there were several reasons behind the disaster that had become Hepburn's career: her failure to spend her riches on glamorous clothes that could in turn be admired and criticized by her fans; her failure to act like a proper movie star; her unavailability for standard interviews with the press; her failure to get married, divorced, go on a bender, do something intriguing; and her perceived snobbery.

There was also something else, something unsettling no one could put a finger on. In those pre-Tracy-and-Hepburn days, Hepburn's scenes with her leading men were simply unconvincing. You can see it in her reviews. The critics were all over the board. Some said Hepburn was a natural but limited genius when it came to playing a certain type of role, others said she was "mannered" and phony, fluttery, jittery, and affected. She seemed unable to play a woman in love with anything approaching conviction, and this was enough in 1938 to unnerve the nation's moviegoers.

Hepburn was the most arch and artificial when she was trying to land her man. All that fluttery, high-voiced, eyelash-batting business; all that simpering, mindless chatter. For most of all her movies, even the patently lousy ones, she strode across the screen, confident and cool and clever. Yet because the culture dictated that a woman must be conquered by love, there was always one patch of wretched acting in every film, a few god-awful minutes in which she fawned and giggled and flapped her hands and rolled her eyes as if a seizure might be coming on. She got called again and again for her coy and mannered behavior, but what no one quite put together was that her inability to realistically portray acceptable feminine behavior was an indictment of the *behavior* and not of the actress. That, of course, was terrifying and thus unacceptable. Better to blame the actress than the demands of the culture.

Audiences were simultaneously intrigued and repelled by Hepburn's sexy, svelte athleticism. Prior to Kate's arrival on the scene, any actress who was remotely sporty was also butch. But Hepburn was lithe and fine-boned. Her waist looked tiny enough to encircle with one hand. Still, her body looked like a tool, like something to be employed and enjoyed—in the service of what, people weren't quite sure; thus the whole haughty, witty, gleaming, long-legged Hepburn package was terrifying.

Long before Gloria Steinem observed that on some level all women are female impersonators, Hepburn was unwittingly showing it to be true. Hepburn *did* have a limited range, and the limit was acting insipid and submissive opposite a leading man who couldn't hold a candle to her. To make matters worse, Hepburn also managed to convey that she had other fish to fry, and there's nothing more dangerous than a woman who can't be brought to her knees by love.

◆—◆

So, what was Hepburn to do? I mean, short of dog breeding and restaurant opening. She was thirty-one years old. What is anyone to do at such a crossroads, when any misstep might mean the end of a career? The obvious lesson is to work hard; but Hepburn always worked hard. In every disappointing movie of the mid-thirties she worked as hard as she knew how.

Among the many unsung ways in which Hepburn was ahead of her time, one was to be a complete workaholic. People seldom appreciate the rigors of moviemaking. Since almost no one in our land would pass up the chance to star in a movie, we assume that there's not much to it besides sitting in a director's chair with your name stitched on the back, waiting for the Craft Services people to bring out the white-chocolate-chip-macadamia-nut cookies and the Red Bull.

Setting aside the many advantages of being an actor who commands starring roles—hefty salary, huge acclaim, variety, not having to wear panty hose or endure the commute—genuine work is involved. Genuine running down the street with your sidearm pulled in pursuit of the guy who knows where the bomb is; genuine fit-pitching when you find out your husband is sleeping with your sister; genuine faux-impromptu singing in the rain. Sometimes, there are many takes of these taxing behaviors.

Hepburn was more of a trouper than most actresses, who were at that time viewed as delicate flowers. Until she was well into her sixties, she did her own stunts. Her slogging through the jungle carrying the production's only mirror during the filming of *The African Queen* is legendary, as is the chronic eye infection she incurred from performing a fake fall into a real polluted Venetian canal during the filming of *Summertime*.

During the filming of *Little Women* the regular sound guys went on strike; anyone in the vicinity who could reliably press the record button was rounded up to pitch in. That day they filmed a scene that required Hepburn to break down sobbing. As in acting, pressing the record button is also not as easy as it sounds; Hepburn was required to do fifteen takes of the scene, after which she threw up from the exertion.

Winning an Oscar was nice in 1934, but it didn't possess nearly the cachet it does today (you could also argue that the Oscar curse was already up and running, working its nefarious and mystical Oscar mojo to make sure that Hepburn's career would hit the skids before the statuette was even delivered). The Academy of Motion Picture Arts and Sciences was still a fledgling nonprofit. It could easily have gone the way of New Coke. The famous accounting firm of Price Waterhouse was yet to be employed to manage the balloting (initiated in 1935). No one said, "The envelope please . . ." (instituted in 1941), and there was no television to broadcast the ceremony into the homes of millions of people. Also, movies were still considered déclassé.

Hepburn had been accused of behaving as if she were slumming in Hollywood, but the fact is, she *was* slumming in Hollywood. She wasn't the only one who thought Hollywood was the entertainment hub on the wrong side of the tracks. New York was the capital of Western civilization, the home of The Theatah. In the same way that several decades ago no serious film actor would get caught dead doing TV, the real actors were on Broadway, and Hepburn believed that her success in films might make it easier to make her way back East.

So back she went to New York, to humiliate herself thoroughly in the aforementioned *The Lake*, directed by the tyrannical Jed Harris. Hepburn was intimidated by her fellow cast members, all stage veterans. One day she showed up for rehearsal in a pair of overalls and men's shirt, and Harris ordered her offstage until she could find a dress. Backstage she fashioned a skirt out of a burlap bag. Everyone had a good laugh at her expense. (It never occurred to her she may have brought this on herself.) Still, she was an Oscar winner, the star of screen, if not stage; I can't imagine Hilary Swank or Reese Witherspoon or any other winner of recent vintage getting laughed offstage on account of her apparel.

When the playwright and critic George S. Kaufman heard that the hyper-nervous Hepburn requested a curtain be hung between the stage and the wings, so she wouldn't be distracted, he said, "She's afraid she might catch acting." More humiliating still was the remark made by Dorothy Parker, then at the height of her fame and snarkiness. She reviewed *The Lake* on opening night and claimed that Hepburn's performance ran the gamut of emotions from A to B. Long after the play tanked, Parker's pan lived on. Years later, when the wounds had healed and Hepburn was being carried around on the world's shoulders for her devotion to Tracy, her many award-winning performances, her refusal to retire gracefully when her neck got too wrinkly, she would say, "Ran the gamut from A to B? Hell, I didn't even make it to B."

The point is—and this is why Hepburn earned a place among the gods—she kept at it. Hepburn kept trying to improve her performance *after* the critics had swept through and rendered their production-closing proclamations, going so far as to hire voice coach Susan Steele to help her work on her shrill and mannered delivery. Even though the critics were long gone, and the audience dwindled with each performance, she worked hard and she got better, and there was no one around to care about it, in the end, but her.

◆—◆

It would be nice if hard work was all it took. Most parents tell their children that if you work hard enough, you'll achieve your dreams. Is this because parents want to believe it's that simple—after all, even someone with no talent or aptitude can work hard—or because it's just too dispiriting to be the one to break the news to a five-year-old that he will most likely never be a professional basketball player, gold-medal-winning gymnast, or Mick Jagger?

Sometime during that dark year, before the hurricane, Hepburn repaired to Fenwick to take stock and figure out how she could turn her fate around. It's always good to have somewhere to go to figure things out, preferably a place that encourages long walks and doesn't require dress shoes. Hepburn swam at the crack of dawn in water cold enough to turn her lips blue, practiced her fancy half-gainers and swan dives, golfed with the locals of Old Saybrook, played tennis until she dropped, clobbered everyone in her family at Parcheesi—her board game of choice—and in general did the things that restored her and, all the while, figured out a few hard truths.

Hard truth #1: She had to stop taking roles that required her to play Ozark faith healers (*Spitfire*); self-destructive composers (*Break of Hearts*); gypsy anarchists who fall in love with men of the cloth (*The Little Minister*); cross-dressing daughters of minor English criminals (*Sylvia Scarlett*), and doomed Scottish queens (*Mary of Scotland*). If she could make a role her own (Jo March in *Little Women*), that was worth considering. Otherwise, from then on, she would only take roles that were written for her.

Hard truth #2: Any roles that were written for her would allow her to express her particular—but unorthodox—genius: embodying self-confident women of privilege who were also beautiful, intelligent, thin, and unlikely to lose their head over some stupid man.

Hard truth #3: This kind of woman is completely loathsome . . .

Hard truth #4: . . . particularly in 1938, when everyone was ragged from the continuing effects of the Depression and the problems of the idle rich were annoying.

Hard truth #5: Given Hard Truths #3 and #4, and her box-office-poison status, it was unlikely she would find anyone to write a role only for her.

◆—◆

Enter playwright Philip Barry, whose career was also on the skids. In the 1930s Barry's sophisticated drawing-room comedies were relics of happier days; his soufflé-light plays celebrated and lampooned the Fifth Avenue stone-mansion crowd, and as we know, by the end of the decade everyone had had enough of them and their martinis.

Barry had had a number of hits on Prohibition-era Broadway, including *Holiday*, which ran for 229 performances in 1928. Ten years later, the film version starred Hepburn and Cary Grant, but the central question of the play—after you've made a boatload of money, should you go on "holiday" or continue to push your rock uphill, amassing as much wealth as possible?—seemed to interest audiences less than it had ten years earlier. The public reception of the 1938 film, directed by George Cukor, is a measure of how much public mood can change in a decade. Even though *Holiday* is routinely considered one of Cukor's best films and includes a revelatory performance by Cary Grant as free-spirited Johnny Case, a working-class guy who falls in love with, yes, an heiress (heiresses were as common in movies of that era as paid assassins are today), *Holiday* was met with indifference.

Philip Barry had always been enthralled by Hepburn's slim, boyish, big-talking mien. When Hepburn approached him about writing a play for her, his last three light comedies hadn't met with much success. Between the two of them, it was difficult to tell who was the most unpopular.

Hepburn cornered him and said, "Make a character like me." A character like *her*? But people could not abide a character like her. It was well documented. Critics and fans alike had grown sick of her shtick—her sense of entitlement, her refusal to hide

her intelligence, her strident mannerisms, and her stubborn disinclination to be pleasing in the traditional feminine manner—but
her shtick was all she had and all she was, and conveying women
who possessed it was what she did better than just about anyone
else. She was sure it was worth betting the house on.

So Hepburn stuck to her knitting, even though at the time
nothing seemed like a worse idea. More impressive, she managed
to coerce Barry to stick to *his* knitting, to write a play about the
travails of the idle rich. "Make her like me, then make her go all
soft," she reputedly instructed Barry. Thus was Tracy Lord and *The
Philadelphia Story* born.

A few decades later Robert Pirsig* would say, "When someone
goes outside the cultural norms, the culture has to protect itself."
Hepburn, notoriously nonanalytical, was all for helping the culture
protect itself, if such protection would give her the freedom to play
women . . . well . . . like herself. She would embody the arrogant
woman who had everything for three fourths of a movie, then
arrange—or allow—her comeuppance, thus allowing her audiences
their schadenfreude, the same way a good mother makes her children finish their broccoli before scooping out the ice cream.

It's the old story; scratch a woman and her love of the messy
warmth of life must be apparent. If she's tough to the core, she remains a freak of nature. Softness in a woman is a necessity, even if

---

*Author of *Zen and the Art of Motorcycle Maintenance* and another person ahead of his
time who, before he became known as a great sage, enjoyed a reputation as a
crackpot.

in terms of her basic survival it's useful mostly as a tool of manipulation. Hepburn had figured out that the only way people would accept the sort of woman she was born to play was if in the last reel she was transformed into a "softie."

The story of Hepburn's comeback sounds like one of her movies, which would one day delight her. Justice has rarely been more poetic. *The Philadelphia Story* ran 415 performances on Broadway and made a million at the box office. (I'm not going to bother to translate that into modern dollars—it's a lot.) Howard Hughes shrewdly thought to buy his ex the film rights, and so when Hollywood wanted to make the movie, they had to deal with her. Hepburn demanded that she reprise her role as the imperious Tracy Lord, and that she have her choice of leading men (she wanted Clark Gable and Spencer Tracy; she got Jimmy Stewart and her old sidekick Cary Grant). She shrewdly deferred her salary for forty-five percent of the profits.

Of the film, the *New York Times* said, "It has been a long time since Hollywood has spent itself so extravagantly, and to such entertaining effect, upon a straight upper-crust fable, an unblushing apologia for plutocracy . . . It is like old times to see one about the trials and tribulations of the rich, and to have Miss Hepburn back, after a two-year recess, as another spoiled and willful daughter of America's unofficial peerage, comporting herself easily amid swimming pools, stables and the usual appurtenances of a huge estate."

◆·◆

It would be unfair if I didn't stop here and qualify a few things. Hepburn was both unique to her time and of her time. In many ways, the nation was more culturally advanced in 1938 than it is today. I don't think I'm alone in confusing technological progress with cultural progress. In 1938, the customer-dialed long-distance phone call was a decade and a half away, but that year movies opened starring Joan Crawford as a nightclub dancer, Bette Davis as a proto–Scarlett O'Hara, Ginger Rogers as a bored New York office worker. Dancer, Southern belle, and pink-collar cube dweller aren't particularly glamorous occupations, and in the end all of them wind up "in love," but in 1938 the story of an average woman's journey was still thought to be enough to carry a narrative. Now, unless the source material is a novel by Steve Martin, no one is interested in the plight of a shopgirl.

The top ten grossing movies from a random week in fall 2006 have no female leads in any of them. Instead there is:

A Bond girl
A mother (a computer-animated penguin)**
Mrs. Claus, who's pregnant
An ex-wife
A girlfriend (a computer-animated sewer rat)*
An assistant to a psychopath
A doctor
A girlfriend
A wife who's been shot**
A nanny

Another wife, who weeps a lot and takes to drink
A magician's assistant*
A disheveled novelist**

To be an actress now—the stated career goal of millions of young girls far and wide—means to be vying for costarring roles as girlfriends, wives, ex-wives, and assistants. If you manage to land a role that is not a love interest, i.e., you have a real profession, you will either be kidnapped and tortured (the doctor), or have let yourself go to such a degree that you're not fit for human companionship (the disheveled novelist).

Of the thirteen roles listed above, two are animated, both voiced by Oscar-caliber actresses. Three of the remaining eleven roles are played by actresses who've either been nominated for, or won, an Oscar. It's a stretch, but not much of one, to say that the sort of feature-film roles available to some of the world's best actresses are Mrs., ex-Mrs., or soon-to-be-Mrs. (fingers crossed!). If you were a thirty-one-year-old actress today, who like Hepburn, had won an Oscar, but had a good half dozen flops behind you, there would be no question about a comeback. Your future would most likely be that reality television show in which D-list celebrities all live together in a big house.

——◆—◆——

*Oscar nominee
**Oscar winner

It wasn't always clear that movies were going to be a license to print money. In the early days, movie people were viewed by the culturati as crackpots, out there in Los Angeles, cranking out cheap entertainment under the mind-numbing sun. Woody Allen's *Purple Rose of Cairo* gets the import of the movies in the Depression just right. Who were the movies for? Depressed New Jersey waitresses, like Mia Farrow's Cecilia, in need of escape from their dull and difficult lives; men also suffered then, of course, but escaping their woes in anything but a bottle or a card game was viewed as unmanly. Adolescent boys had not yet become Hollywood's preferred target audience. Indeed, no one knew from target audiences or focus groups. In many ways, it was an innocent time.

5

THE IMPRACTICALITY OF MARRIAGE

*Marriage as a Series of Desperate Arguments; The Ideal Male and the Ideal
Female as Represented by Tracy and Hepburn; The Laws of Cohabitation;
Opting out of Marriage; Opting out of Everything but Marriage;
Choice Equals Sacrifice*

The top-grossing movie of 1942 was *Woman of the Year*, starring
Spencer Tracy and Katharine Hepburn. It was always Tracy
and Hepburn, instead of the other way around, which would have
made more sense from both an alphabetical and a ladies-first perspective. When asked why he wouldn't allow Hepburn top billing,
Tracy replied, "This is a movie, not a lifeboat."

Woman of the Year was a romantic comedy, but it was also a
documentary chronicling the early goo-goo eyes stage of one of
Hollywood's greatest love affairs. On-screen, Tracy and Hepburn
cannot get enough of each other. Some scenes are so intimate,
you must look away. In the handful of chaste kisses, Tracy steps
between Hepburn and the camera; she is hidden from the audience by the hulking frame of this man who will be the love of her

life. The film critic for the *New York Times*, Bosley Crowther, said, "Miss Hepburn projects a surprising warmth which she had not heretofore seemed to possess." Of course. Love softened Hepburn, just as it does everyone else. Fortunately, after a while, it hardens you right back up, like a chocolate bar left overnight on the dashboard.

◆—◆—◆

Even though Hepburn's lone experience with matrimony consisted of her short, lusterless union to the affable Luddy, she considered herself an expert on the topic. And why not? Hepburn loved nothing more than pulling the pin out of the grenade with her teeth and hurling it into the accepted mores of the time. Her attitude toward marriage was complicated, which in those times was tantamount to saying you were antimarriage.

In the middle of last century, when every girl was supposed to regard marriage as her highest achievement—not unlike today, the pendulum having swung rather alarmingly back into the age of June Cleaver—Hepburn said that if it wasn't bloody impractical to love, honor, and obey, you wouldn't have to sign a contract. She wondered whether men and women truly suited each other, suggested that they should instead live next door and visit now and then. In a pensée that could have been cribbed from Mae West's daybook, she also said, "If you want to sacrifice the admiration of many men for the criticism of one, go ahead, get married!"

One wonders why Hepburn had so much to say about marriage,

since she'd made it clear on a number of occasions that the whole thing simply wasn't for her. Could it be she made so much noise about marriage because she was never quite sure where she stood on the issue? It's one of the endearing quirks of human nature that we often say something aloud not to convince other people, but to convince ourselves. Maybe Hepburn kept taking another run at a simple, all-embracing philosophy of love and marriage in order to settle the matter in her mind once and for all. I suspect that like most of us, she was ambivalent.

After her marriage to Luddy dissolved and she was involved with her agent, Leland Hayward, she refused his offer of marriage several times, only to be insulted and heartbroken when he married Margaret Sullavan. If she was truly antimarriage, why did she care? Her answer was no less inexplicable than ours would be: she cared because she just did.

Or, maybe Hepburn was a true radical. In today's America if a star of Hepburn's wattage went on record as saying the promises of marriage were bloody impractical, she would be accused of trying to destroy the morals of the nation.

The lesson to be gleaned here is heartening: if you are confused about the man/woman thing (or the man/man thing, or the woman/woman thing), take heart. The mighty Hepburn, so sure about so many other things in life, was just as flummoxed as the rest of us when it came to the eternal questions of dating, mating, and cohabitating.

◆–◆–◆

Hepburn is said to have said, "Marriage is a series of desperate arguments people feel passionate about." As with many Hepburnisms, the provenance of this bon mot is unknown. It sounds so good, so kitchen-sampler right, it doesn't even matter that it's not true. I'm a lifelong fan of the bold metaphor, but marriage as a series of desperate arguments? Hepburn makes matrimony sound like a good production of *Waiting for Godot*, which, come to think of it, it sort of is. The arguments of an individual partnership may start out desperate and passionate, but over time they tend to devolve into habitual bickering. *Do you have to be so controlling? Why do you always have to overspend at Christmas? Here, let me introduce you to the laundry hamper. Why do I have to ask you seven times to take out the garbage? Why do you have to leave those nubby beard hairs in the sink after you shave? Could we be on time for once? Can't you tell your brother no? Why do you have to hog the remote? Yes, you do snore.*

Still, Hepburn's thought is enigmatic enough to be of interest. It sounds born of experience. But her marriage to the good-natured Luddy was anything but desperately argumentative or passionate, even in the early days of their courtship when the uninhibited Hepburn posed nude for her future husband, an enthusiastic amateur photographer.

By all reports Luddy was agreeable, meek, somewhat fey, and in possession of his own car.* His favorite party trick was touching the end of his nose with his tongue. Hepburn's family loved him

---

*Big doings in 1928.

because they saw immediately that he was genial enough to allow himself to be bullied by Kate.

One Luddy and Hepburn legend goes like this: before they wed, Hepburn asked him to change his name from Ludlow Ogden Smith to Ogden Smith Ludlow so she wouldn't have to suffer being confused with Kate Smith, the zaftig singer a mere eleven days older than Hepburn herself, who in 1931 enjoyed a hit record, the alarmingly titled "That's Why Darkies Were Born," but who was otherwise not *fascinating*, Hepburn's favorite adjective for herself.

Most likely the name change happened long after they were married, but in any case Luddy complied without a fuss, even though his mother, a staunch Philadelphia Main Line battle-ax, was livid. So benign and good-natured was Luddy that even after Hepburn left him to pursue her acting career in Hollywood, eventually seeking a quickie Mexican divorce, he was still magnanimous enough to invest in the Broadway production of *The Philadelphia Story*.

✦━◆━✦

Marriage may not have been a series of desperate arguments for Katharine Hepburn Ludlow and Ogden Smith Ludlow, but it certainly was for Tess Harding Craig (Hepburn) and Sam Craig (Tracy), in *Woman of the Year*. I come back to this because it's where it all began.

The day before filming Tracy and Hepburn met for the first

time, and she (five feet seven inches, plus heels) said to him (five feet ten inches, give or take), "I'm afraid I'm too tall for you, Mr. Tracy." To which he replied, "Don't worry, I'll cut you down to size." That's not the way it went, actually. The producer Joseph Mankiewicz was standing there, feeling like the third wheel. *He* was the one who said it. Tracy, apparently, just stared at Hepburn. When it comes to pretty much all matters Tracy/Hepburn, the world prefers the legend to the truth, which was far from witty.

Woman of the Year concerns itself with the romance between two newspaper columnists, international affairs expert Tess Harding, played by a luminous Hepburn, whose astonishing svelteness presaged the look of generations of supermodels to come, and lumpen sports columnist Sam Craig, played by Spencer Tracy, who is as weathered and lined as a clay-animated caveman.

Tess is modern with a capital *M*—flighty, charming, distracted, and wed to her Teletype machine (in a remake it would be her BlackBerry), from which she gleans late-breaking global news. She has a swanky Fifth Avenue apartment, a wardrobe of chic hats, and a male personal assistant. World leaders routinely consult her on matters of state, and she's fluent in Chinese, Russian, and Greek. In contrast, Tracy's Sam is a salt-of-the-earth, no-nonsense straight talker who's got his priorities straight (as if complex international peace accords and civil wars in the developing world are silly women's business and the current state of the Yankees' bullpen is grave and manly, and therefore serious and worthwhile).

Opposites attract, and their marriage becomes one long,

hilarious, desperate argument about the way in which Tess takes every opportunity possible to put her career above her man. No chance to display her shocking selfishness is overlooked by director George Stevens. In one hilarious shot Tess is lying in Sam's arms, striving mightily to evince interest in a college football game he's just covered. He's holding a newspaper and has an arm around her in such a way that she can read her own column, which she does, so much more interesting does she find one of her already published opinions than his explanation of why there are no innings in football.

The neglected Sam leaves Tess, and in the final scene she tries to win him back by attempting to make him a waffle in her mink coat. In the background a tightly wound toaster shoots squares of toast into the air, and on the stove the tarlike coffee boils over. He silently watches her dismal cooking skills until she collapses into tears, at which point he takes her in his arms and consoles for her ineptitude; she tried, after all! They hug, and the credits roll.

I almost wrote, "Despite the ridiculous ending, the scene is still hilarious," forgetting that in our current times many women wouldn't find this to be ridiculous at all. It's come to make a depressing amount of sense that all a brilliant, accomplished woman has to do to keep her man happy is confine herself to the kitchen. What might now seem objectionable is that Tess wears mink.

The original ending—now lost—had Sam and Tess at a baseball game, with Tess cheering like a maniac alongside her approving hubby. He's won her over to his side; she's a bigger fan than he is. Preview audiences didn't like this. It wasn't enough. The pie she was made to eat was too reasonable, too equitable, not humble enough. She needed to be punished for speaking all those languages and having a passion for foreign policy and not knowing how long to cook a soft-boiled egg. Women needed to see her struggle at that which they could do in their sleep—throw together a ranch hand's breakfast for Mr. Right.

Hepburn is said to have despised the ending, but she went along with it. She had learned her lesson from the success of *The Philadelphia Story*. People loved her as long as she agreed in the final reel to eat a little humble pie.

—•—•—

Director George Stevens said of Tracy and Hepburn's immediate and enduring chemistry, "Spence's reaction to Kate was a total, pleasant, but glacial put-down of her extreme effusiveness. He just didn't get disturbed about doing things immediately; she wanted to do a hundred and one things at once; he was never in a hurry."

Shrewd Hepburn understood their intrinsic appeal at once. "On-screen Spencer and I are the perfect American couple," she said. "I needle him. I irritate him. I try to get around him. If he put a big paw on my head, he could squash me. I think this is the romantic, ideal picture of the male and female in this country."

HOW TRACY EMBODIES THE IDEAL MALE	HOW HEPBURN EMBODIES THE IDEAL FEMALE
Large head (indicates he "has a good head on his shoulders")	Small head (lack of seriousness)
Doesn't say much (great depth)	Talkative, witty (annoying)
Gruff and inflexible (strong, committed)	Intelligent, traffics in complex ideas (European, untrustworthy)
Sports loving (appreciation of what's truly important in life)	Wonders why football doesn't have innings (see "small head," above)
Small, dingy teeth that look as if they could use a brushing (lack of interest in superficialities)	Perfect white choppers (anything less would be a character flaw)
Favors one kind of hat (Protective . . . when not squashing your head with his big paw)	Wears a number of silly hats (provokes desire to squash head)

►—•—◄

Between 1942 and 1967 Tracy and Hepburn made nine movies together, some of which are still worth seeing—besides *Woman of the
Year*, there's *State of the Union* (1948), *Adam's Rib* (1949), *Pat and
Mike* (1952), *Desk Set* (1957), and *Guess Who's Coming to Dinner*
(1967)—and some of which stank up the joint. The ones we love
best are not unlike contemporary war movies, where the audience
is allowed the illicit thrill of watching cities get torched and the
enemy blown in half, safe in the knowledge that the film will end
with the message that war is hell. Audiences could abandon themselves to the thrill of the superior Hepburn stalking through the
scenes, pantherlike, controlling her life and the direction of the
conversation, knowing that she wouldn't get away with this for
long. In *Woman of the Year* it would be unthinkable for Tess and
Sam Craig to split after three or four years, realizing that they were
simply too different, that she needed someone more sophisticated, and he needed someone less.

    This, of course, is how it usually turns out in real life.

◆—◆—◆

Hepburn's staunch I'm Just Not the Marrying Kind philosophy was
outré in the forties and fifties; prescient in the sixties; trendsetting
in the seventies; and finally, now, smacking of some arthritic feminist notion that fell out of style with bra-burning and fondue
(although I hear fondue is making a comeback).

    Everyone is the marrying kind these days, with the exception of George Clooney.* The time when self-knowledge might include the realization (sad or otherwise) that you're just not meant for marriage, homeownership, or skinny jeans is behind us. We are living in an age of unmitigated entitlement. We want what we want, and what we want is everything we can reasonably get our hands on—absorbing work, money rolling in, the overheated love of pop songs, marriage, fine children, adorable pets, intriguing vacations, Spanish pavers for the backyard patio, even a regular shift ladling out chili at a local soup kitchen, the better to reassure ourselves that our lives also have meaning.

Because it's not uncommon to own a car longer than a spouse, marriage isn't the one-way turnstile it once was. It's a thing people can have for a while, like a time-share in Puerto Vallarta. I feel a bit wistful that this is so, but marriage has become just another phase, like dyeing your hair blue, that comes when you're suddenly overwhelmed with the urge to experience the cozy rush of shopping for throw pillows and pillar candles at Pottery Barn, sharing a bed, a tax return, and a collection of excruciating holidays.

Admitting, as Hepburn did, that you cannot have a full-time career that consumes your every waking moment *and* a family, who

---

*Clooney is sort of a male Hepburn for the modern age. There's his devotion to privacy, the mystery surrounding his love life, his intelligence and wit, unique sense of personal style, iconoclastic movie career, and eccentricities, one of which he displayed recently when he publicly grieved the death of Max, his three hundred-pound Chinese potbellied pig, who is rumored to have shared Clooney's bed, thus making him the envy of millions.

might also consume a considerable amount of time and energy, is viewed as pessimistic, unsporting, or cowardly. Even though we value self-knowledge, *this* sort of self-knowledge—at least for a woman—that maybe you don't have the desire or inclination to have it all or do it all, is considered selfish, lazy, even traitorous. Knowing our limitations is un-American.

Hepburn was no stranger to self-delusion and denial (see chapter 7), but she did understand some immutable facts about the realities of cohabitation and marriage, laws of domesticity that it would behoove everyone to understand and accept *before* you register at Williams-Sonoma or launch your Look Who's Getting Married! Web site.

First Law of Domesticity: The Person Who Cares the Most Will Do the Most

This applies to the mess, the nature and quality of the meals, the décor, the way the fitted sheets are folded, everything domestic you can think of. The impulse to leap to the assumption that (heterosexual) men are just slobs must be resisted. Remove the question of gender, and the principle still applies. A recent Dilbert cartoon nailed the entire concept in three panels: a pair of messy coworkers left their dirty plates out, waiting for "a loser with higher standards" to come by and pick them up.

In a college-dorm quad occupied by four guys, the one the most repulsed by green fur growing in the toilet is the one who will wind up most often on his hands and knees with the scrub brush. In marriage, the wife usually cares more. She is the loser with higher standards. Whether nature or nurture is responsible, who can say, but the simple fact is that unless you're a bred-in-the-bone slob (and messier than your husband) or you've had the good fortune to fall in love and marry the guy in the quad who took it upon himself to scrub the toilet, you're looking at doing most of the housework.

Second Law of Domesticity: You Cannot Force Someone to Care About the Rank Leftovers at the Back of the Fridge

In the same way that the tidiest guy in the quad cannot in any meaningful, permanent way affect the habits of the roommate who hasn't worn clean underwear since he lived at home, so, too, wives will never be able to get even the best husbands to participate in the so-called Second Shift without resorting to coercion, manipulation, nagging, shrieking, pleading, sulking, brightly colored chore charts, hurling crockery, withholding sex, or threatening to do the pool boy.

Men may care whether the inside of their car is clean; they may not like anyone to mess with their CD collection or touch their L.A. Raiders memorabilia, but they're less concerned about the order and cleanliness of the general living areas. If they've managed to stay married, they are too smart to have come right out and said, "Hey, hon, the fridge, and all the leftovers that have taken up permanent residency in the back—that's your department." Still, on some level they believe it—in much the same way that when they're watching the kids, they call it "babysitting," as if these youngsters belong to the neighbors.

However, the good husbands will dig out the nasty leftovers if we ask them to. But know this: they wouldn't do it if they lived alone. And just because they do it once because you've asked them, this will not be the beginning of a trend. They are only doing it because you pestered them, and they do love you. They also love keeping the peace. But they could not give a fig about the ancient lo mein creating a health hazard on the third shelf. They don't care now, nor will they ever care.

Hepburn understood this reality. She also understood the peculiar position competent wives have found themselves in since Ruth gleaned the barley fields of Boaz. "I can carry the logs up from the cellar and build a fire," Hepburn said. "But if I were married to someone and I did this, and he was sitting reading the paper, I would like him to feel that he's a lazy son of a bitch." She is, of course, speaking of the resentment that takes root in a relationship when the husband, who cares less (First Law) and cannot be forced to care more (Second Law), goes about his business while the wife endlessly attends.

Because Hepburn both wanted her fire and didn't want to resent a man she loved (in this case, Spencer Tracy) for not building the fire himself, she opted out of marriage. She also wanted to hit the road when she felt like it. Throughout her long liaison with Tracy, whenever she got the hankering to, say, take off for Australia to star in *Taming of the Shrew*, she could, and no one would think less of her. It is one of the distinct advantages of being the mistress rather than the wife.

If the recent flurry of lifestyle reports is true, young women today are also opting out, not of marriage but of having a life outside it. And who can blame them? If they can land a man—for purposes of this discussion I'm going to root around at the back of the linguistic cupboard and dust off some terms from 1955—who'll pick up the check for the rest of their adult lives, they are to be commended. They are realists. They know better than to fight city hall: they know that regardless of whether they're the CEO of Hewlett-Packard or the head of the wrapping-paper fund-raiser at Fruit 'n Flower preschool, they're still going to be the ones in charge of the house, the children, and making the dental appointments (seventy-five percent of all dental appointments made in America are made by women, for their family).

These Shrewd Young Things have learned from watching their ambitious, overachieving big sisters dash around like women hooked on meth that the reward for doing everything is the privilege of continuing to do everything. Virtue is its own reward and its only reward. It is the curse of competence. They have watched these older women collect husbands, high-powered jobs, houses, and children as if they were Fiesta ware, and still this has not resulted in complete fulfillment but an exhaustion so deep that they long not for a vacation (have you ever taken three children on vacation?) but a bite of Snow White's apple, the better to have a nice long rest.

A fun statistic: when women marry, the amount of housework they do goes up thirty-three percent; when men marry, the amount they do goes down seventeen percent. And that's on a good day.

Given this, *who needs it?* A job, I mean. Have a nice day at work, honey, I'll be at Pilates.

The lifestyle reports—many of which have appeared in the *New York Times*—are most fascinated when the great, privileged masses of female Harvard M.B.A.s (Yale law graduates, Johns Hopkins medical residents, etc.) opt out. They care less about the young woman who earned her B.A. at Cal State Fullerton or U Albany, for whom opting out isn't a choice but a luxury, like a cashmere hoodie.

This, too, is understandable. We are suckers for stories of great extravagance and wasted resources, and nothing strikes us as more delightfully wasteful than an Ivy League education put in the service of picking up toys from the living room floor six times a day. What no one dares say, although the subtext is clear, is that if these devoted wives and moms aren't going to use their high-priced educations, perhaps they should give their spot to a deserving man who will one day be expected to support their sorry, if toned, ass.

But I digress.

The point is, both the ultra-independent Hepburn and meal-ticket-seeking Shrewd Young Thing understand that choice, by its very nature, involves a sacrifice.

◆—◆

This is the part where I should say that the lesson is pick one thing—all right, maybe two, I'm no less greedy than everyone else—commit to it, and do it well.

Look the realities of life hard in the eye. You only have so much time. You only have so much energy. You've got the kinks and quirks of your own God-given personality with which to contend.

If you make your sole occupation your marriage, know there are risks, one of which is resentment. You will do most if not all of the work at home and in the relationship.* The day will come when you will carry the wood up from the cellar and make the fire and your husband will be sitting reading the paper, or watching ESPN *SportsCenter*, or playing a video game with your sons (his concept of parenting), and you will think he's a lazy son of a bitch. You may get dumped for the personal assistant, the nanny, the FedEx girl, and then where will you be, you who let your jobs skills expire as casually as if they were a coupon for a free latte. Even if you're blessed, and your marriage is one of the rare over-the-top terrific ones, the stuff of a Cialis ad, with you and your husband waltzing in the meadow at sunset, your children will still want nothing to do with you as soon as they hit middle school, and soon after that they'll be off to college, and then where will you be? They'll have a name for you, and it won't be Shrewd Young Thing, it will be Empty Nester.

If you don't marry a man, but marry a career, know there are risks, one of which is loneliness. You will wind up with too many pets and a lot of empty hours in which to lie on your stomach and peer into the existential abyss of your own mortality. Look at you,

---

*A joke: women may be able to fake orgasms but men can fake entire relationships.

with your fat 401(k), crow's-feet, and no progeny. You'll worry that whoever said "At the end of the day no one wishes she'd spent less time with her family and more time at the office" was right. Your career may become tedious. You may be phased out, outsourced, laid off, or realize the futility of spending your days making someone else rich, or even making yourself rich. One of the joys of money is being able to lavish it on guess who? Your children.

Fortunately the real lesson here has nothing to do with choosing one thing over another. You'll choose one thing or the other thing, with great thought, or none at all, but in the end, as they say at the old Monty Python World Headquarters, "No one expects the Spanish Inquisition."

How could Katharine Hepburn have imagined that at the ripe age of thirty-five she would realize that while she didn't believe in marriage, she did believe in slavish devotion to a married man?

6

MAKING THE MOST OF A
DYSFUNCTIONAL RELATIONSHIP

The Tracy/Hepburn Sizzle; The Audience Is Vindicated; "My Kate"; The Power
of Discretion; Spencer Tracy Is as Troubled as He Is Gifted; What Would
Dr. Phil Say?; The Mystery of Love and Attachment; Love Makes Kate Great

Even though Tracy and Hepburn fell in love during the height of their popularity and physical beauty, the love-shack phase of the affair—about five years—lasted no longer than it does for the average pair of lovers. It's a heartening thought that even the famous and rich are subject to lust's wilting bloom.

Still, between *Woman of the Year* (1942) and *Adam's Rib* (1949) the world was treated to some impressive sizzle. Part of their colossal appeal was that audiences *knew* something *had* to be going on, while, of course, at the time knowing very well that *nothing* could be going on, because Tracy was A Married Man with a Deaf Son, and also a Devout Roman Catholic.

Still, what to make of those simmering gazes? Those effortless riffs of teasing banter? The hot scene in *Woman of the Year* where Hepburn's Tess Harding pauses on the stair to coyly arrange her stocking, while slinging some smart-alecky remark at Tracy's Sam Craig, panting with hat in hand, two risers down? Ooh-la-la.

This could not be a simple demonstration of fine acting. Even today, we don't believe on-screen chemistry is something that can be faked. In a recent review of the new James Bond, attention is paid to whether there is "obvious chemistry" between Bond and his latest girl. So firmly do we believe in the magic of on-screen chemistry, if there is said to be no chemistry between leading lady and man, it's considered bad casting, not bad acting.

For decades hence not much was known about what went on between Tracy and Hepburn. It was said to be an open secret in Hollywood, but they remained as discreet and disciplined as a pair of top-notch father confessors. In 1960, when Hepburn traveled with Tracy to Berlin, where he was filming *Judgment at Nuremberg*, she asked their driver to pull over six blocks from the Hilton, so that she and Tracy might make separate entrances. They had been together eighteen years by then.

No one knew the true depth of their attachment. After Tracy died in 1967, gossip columnist Louella Parsons called it "the greatest love story never told." In 1962, *Look* magazine published a revealing interview with Spencer Tracy, who referred to Hepburn as "my Kate." My Kate! For twenty years she had officially been nothing more than his costar and good friend. Audiences were thrilled; they felt vindicated. (I know my mother was.) They knew true love when they saw it. All those adoring glances. The part in

Pat and Mike where Tracy famously comments on the quality of Hepburn's pulchritude. The part in *Adam's Rib* where they bicker in the car and he makes teasing fun of her Bryn Mawr accent. It was all love all the time, wasn't it? Wasn't it? The world was so thrilled at having its convictions confirmed, it rather overshadowed the matter of Tracy's being a Married Man.

If Tracy and Hepburn were forgiven their cardinal sin, it was because they were so discreet for so many decades. They were discreet for a decade and a half *beyond* the love-shack phase, and into the early 1960s, when poor Tracy's heart, liver, and lungs were failing and Hepburn was more nursemaid than paramour. They were discreet long after the illicit affair was an illicit affair. They snuck around for the sake of appearances, staying in separate hotels and never venturing out in public. By the time Tracy made his public confession, they really were merely costars and good friends.

Or so the thinking goes. Like the existence of extraterrestrial life, no one knows for sure. Neither one kept diaries, confessed the intimate details of their private lives to their friends or correspondents, or thought it appropriate, when their careers needed a boost, to pen a memoir detailing anything remotely resembling an erotic awakening/spiritual journey/chronology of their experiences of adultery. Tracy and Hepburn knew how to keep a secret, and the world rewarded them for it with unconditional adoration. They were what used to be called a class act.

A Primer on How to Be a Class Act

- No matter what, maintain your own address, where your toothbrush and your paid live-in female companion and cook reside.

- Avoid the use of technology. This was easier in 1942 than it is today, but it was also easier to be classy then than now. This means no e-mails, text messages, cell phone calls. Why do you think they still have pay phones? Use them.

- Since none of the methods of communication available to the rest of the world will be available to you and your costar and good friend, arrange to star in a movie together. Days on a movie set are so long you will practically be living together. Tracy and Hepburn were always the first ones on the set in the morning, leaving them plenty of time to steal away into one of the back-lot medieval villages or western saloons for some private time.

- If you and your secret sweetie are not able to land costarring roles in a movie, consider obtaining positions on the same offshore oil rig.

- Since you must never be seen in public, cultivate one wealthy, discreet friend who loves to entertain. Make sure he has a mansion (with swimming pool) where you can hang out for hours on end and pretend you are really a married couple. This will help relieve the stress of never being able to go to Applebee's and hold hands across the table.

○ Understand that despite the rise of reality TV, YouTube, and naked pictures of just about everyone you can imagine floating around the Internet, there is still such a thing as a private life. Honor it.

◆━◆

Spencer Tracy enjoyed a reputation as a somewhat provocative bad boy from the wrong side of the tracks, but he was actually a bad boy of the staunch midwestern middle class. His father, John, was an Irish-American truck salesman who made sure Tracy went to college, and his mother, Caroline, was a homemaker. There were no such things as anger issues, so when Tracy acted out, he was just being a boy. He tasted beer for the first time when he was ten, and that was the beginning of his famous walleyed fits. Once, as a boy, enraged over something or other, Tracy nearly burned the house down. His mother told the police he'd been experimenting with cigarettes. He was expelled from fifteen different grade schools for picking fights. By the time Tracy was a young man enrolled in the American Academy of Dramatic Arts (they accepted him because they were in desperate need of "good masculine types"), he had what in more polite times was called "a drinking problem." Jimmy Cagney would call him the most difficult son of a bitch he'd ever known.

It's a challenge to think of an actor working today with whom to compare Spencer Tracy. The best I can come up with is Russell Crowe on a calm day crossed with the Robert De Niro of *Godfather II*. Tracy's great gift was that he never looked as if he was acting. Watch even the worst of the seventy-four movies he appeared in, and whatever is going wrong on-screen or in the script, it never has anything to do with Tracy. Compare Tracy's performance as John Macreedy, the one-armed war veteran who shows up at a desert backwater that hasn't seen a visitor in four years in *Bad Day at Black Rock* (1955) with that of Burt Lancaster in *The Rainmaker*, where Lancaster starred opposite Hepburn as the flamboyant, madly gesticulating con man Starbuck. Lancaster can't deliver a single line without crouching, leaping, or swinging around a post, as if he'd been cut from the chorus of *Oklahoma!* Indeed, all the male leads throw themselves around (off and on their horses, up and down the porch steps, in and out the front door) as if their acting coach were Dane Cook on speed. *The Rainmaker* is as dated as an old dance card. Tracy's Oscar-nominated performance in *Black Rock*, on the other hand, looks as if it were turned in last week. His low-key gravitas, not to say normal behavior (notice the way he keeps his arms down?) is timeless. Tracy would grumble at the comparison, but he was the little black dress of mid-twentieth-century actors.

Tracy was able to play men of different races, classes, and temperaments with ease. The acting was all in his eyes. He won back-to-back Oscars (1937 and 1938) for his portrayal of a curmudgeonly, curly-headed Portuguese fisherman in *Captains Courageous* and an intrepid priest in *Boys Town*. Tracy would play a lot of priests, a lot of cads, a lawyer (*Inherit the Wind*), a judge (*Judgment at Nuremberg*), and a man wrongly sentenced to die in the electric chair in his first box office hit, *20,000 Years in Sing Sing.*

Tracy's greatest role, however, was that of a pious Roman Catholic who would not divorce his wife for any of his (many!) ladies on the side. A famous quip, attributed to Joseph Mankiewicz, went, "Nobody at MGM gets more sex than Joan Crawford and Spencer Tracy, and that includes the times they get it together." This is not to say that Tracy didn't love his faith. He just loved other things more, including the guilt he felt when he went on a bender or found himself in a compromising position with a starlet. Hepburn wasn't his first lady on the side, nor would she be the last; other Tracy in-amoratas include the gorgeous and girly girls Hedy Lamarr, Loretta Young, Gene Tierney, Ingrid Bergman, and Grace Kelly.

Louise Treadwell and Spencer Tracy were married in 1923 when he was twenty-three and she was twenty-seven. She was not Catholic, but Episcopalian. By all reports she was modest, faithful, serious, and disinclined to suffer Tracy's antics. Nine months after Mr. and Mrs. Tracy were married, she gave birth to their son, John. Ten months later they discovered the boy was deaf, which triggered Tracy's first monumental drunken binge. Tracy is said to have felt enormous guilt over his son's condition, guilt that he'd caused it, guilt that he could not cure it, guilt that the boy's mother, from whom he was eventually estranged, gave her life to the cause of his deafness, founding the John Tracy Clinic, which to this day still operates in Southern California, offering its services free to the families of children with hearing loss. David Niven liked to refer to the saintly Mrs.

Tracy as "the pope." Tracy could not possibly divorce this paragon of virtue, but he could live separately from her and carry on a two-and-a-half-decade-long pseudomarriage with Katharine Hepburn.

◆—◆

Once, in the 1950s, an actress named Jean Porter, wife of Edward Dmytryk, who'd directed Tracy in several of his lesser movies, asked the actor if it was true that he'd never left Louise and married Kate because of his faith. Tracy is said to have said, "Hell no, I wanted to divorce Louise and marry her when we first met, but that's when John was a young kid and had all these problems. I wanted him to have a secure family support system until he got old enough to be on his own, but by that time Kate didn't want to marry me anymore, so we just kept going the way we were going."

And what way would that be?

It was a relationship that would have tickled Karl Marx: from each according to her abilities, to each according to his needs. Hepburn gave so selflessly that were theirs not an adulterous situation, she would qualify for beatification. When the nature of their affair began to surface, and it came out that she used to rush from one Los Angeles watering hole to the next in the dead of an orange-blossom-scented night, trying to track down her beloved before he hurt someone or broke something, her stock climbed higher, not unlike the rise in the approval rating of First Lady Hillary Clinton when she refused to kick her silly philandering husband to the curb.

I wish I didn't have to deliver this lesson, but here it is: if you are a competent woman who threatens everyone around you with your ability to get things done, and you're feeling in need of some familial/societal approval, stand by your erring man for an instant dose of goodwill. The world is arranged thus: people feel kindly toward a good woman who stands by her less-than-good man.*

What must be called Hepburn and Tracy's peculiar dynamic established itself during the filming of that first movie. Midway through production, Tracy, the Ideal Male, sports loving, with his gruff demeanor, few words, large paws, and Flintstonian physique, disappeared on a bender. Hepburn, frantic, prowled his known drinking haunts (yes, even this early into the relationship she already knew them). When she finally found him, she dragged him home and put him to bed.

Hepburn was smitten. Here was the kind of man's man she couldn't resist. She loved his large, leonine noggin, his stocky frame, the matter-of-fact way he treated her enthusiasms, the great respect he enjoyed as an actor "of a good masculine type."

Lauren Bacall said, "She just adored him. It was the only time Katie stopped talking, because she was always hanging on his every word. She was like a twelve-year-old girl sitting at his feet looking at him in wonder."

Hepburn fashioned her life around Tracy's movie roles and drinking binges. They lived in separate houses (he in the guesthouse of director George Cukor), but she managed both households,

---

*Otherwise known as enabling.

seeing to Tracy's cooking, cleaning, chauffeuring, entertaining, and, as Tracy's health worsened, nursing.*

Her other full-time project was keeping him away from the bottle. When Tracy and Hepburn weren't working, she became a camp counselor, and he her lone, doted-upon camper. She kept him busy with art projects, books, stimulating conversation, gallons of coffee, and daily swims. When he was working and she wasn't, she would drive him to the studio, wait on the set, then drive him home and cook him dinner. The flow of concern went in one direction, and one direction only, from Hepburn to Tracy; it was understood that he had his own problems, and they were paramount to hers. When Tracy was slated to film *The Devil at 4 O'Clock* on location on Martinique (Tracy plays another one of his priests; Frank Sinatra plays a convict; together they find themselves marooned on a desert island working at a children's leper colony. The thing sank like a stone), Hepburn took herself to the island ahead of time to find him a comfortable house. She always carried his luggage. And here was one thing I never understood: he let her. Wouldn't a man's man, a good masculine type, insist on carrying *her* luggage?

Tracy treated Hepburn like week-old birthday cake. He called

---

*I would be remiss if I failed to point out that Hepburn, while she did possess the energy of ten men, could only care for Tracy this way because she had people to care for her. She was more wifely than the average wife, but unlike the average wife she had someone to tend to her. She would leave Tracy at night and go home to her companion—the most enduring one was Phyllis—who would have made sure her dinner was ready and waiting. It's somewhat easier to be a selfless caretaker when you don't have a pot of Top Ramen, which you've boiled yourself, facing you at the end of the day.

her Olive Oyl. He called her Bag of Bones. He was known to tell her to just shut the hell up. Hepburn put up no defense, but she did claim that Tracy's "teasing" proved his great affection for her. If Spencer Tracy didn't like you, he just ignored you. Hepburn grew up surrounded on both sides by brothers; maybe she was right.

What is one to do when one loves a real, card-carrying tortured soul? When the spirit moved Spencer Tracy (no other concrete explanation is available), he'd pack a suitcase with Irish whiskey and check into a seedy hotel under his nom de bad boy, Ivan Catchanzoff, for a weeklong drunk. He liked to get sauced in the tub, from which he wouldn't budge for days (not a great visual for fans of the great actor, I'm afraid). He was not a genial drunk. His usual wry, if taciturn, demeanor could devolve into sullen nastiness without warning. Once he punched out a studio employee who dared park in his parking place. Devastated by the premature death of Jean Harlow (at twenty-six, from uremic poisoning), Tracy pitched a fit and tried to toss his brother, Carroll, out the window of his room at the Beverly Wilshire hotel. He occasionally disappeared from the set in the middle of filming, forcing the production to shut down until he turned up again. If the studio publicists were to be believed, Spencer Tracy suffered from more pneumonia than any dozen people put together. Still, Tracy could be funny. He starred in an ill-conceived movie with Hedy Lamarr called *I Take This Woman*, which he nicknamed *I Retake This Woman*.

At the end of the forties, Tracy and Hepburn's relationship fell into a new pattern. Hepburn was still consumed with Tracy's well-being—she would be until his death in 1967—but she realized she really needed to get out more. Unlike Tracy, who liked nothing more than to hole up in his small bungalow and read detective novels, Hepburn possessed the travel bug. She loved a good challenge. Tracy was a good challenge, but Kate could only chauffeur him around, brew him endless cups of tea, encourage his interest in watercolors and do all the other things she did to keep him away from whiskey, for so long. Then, she needed to get the hell out of there for a bit, to feel the dust of the world upon her feet. She needed to make a movie in Africa, or go to Australia for the summer with the Old Vic to do a little Shakespeare, or star in a play in London or New York. She needed a break.

Tracy was not keen on any of this. Every time Hepburn took off, he pouted. And given Hepburn's devotion to his every need, who can blame him? The minute her train chugged out of the station, he broke open the bottle, and sometimes took up with another actress, just for spite. A flurry of phone calls would follow, in which Tracy let Hepburn hear for herself how bad he was doing without her, and in which Hepburn would suggest a nice long walk or a swim. She never told him to stop drinking. Later, she would say she never brought up the subject of Alcoholics Anonymous because she doubted he would have been able to make it, and anyway he was Spencer Tracy. There would have been nothing anonymous about it, and it would have ended his career. Instead, Hepburn would enlist the help of George Cukor, Tracy's landlord, penning urgent missives asking him to tiptoe down to the "old man's" guesthouse and check up on him to make sure he was all right, that he hadn't passed out or died.

In 1951, after *The African Queen* wrapped in the Belgian Congo,

Hepburn and Humphrey Bogart were expected in London for an additional six weeks of filming. Tracy agreed to meet her there, and when her arrival was delayed, he asked out actress Joan Fontaine, whom he'd met at a dinner party. In the summer of 1957, when Hepburn appeared in *Much Ado About Nothing* at the Stratford, Connecticut, Shakespeare theater, Tracy promised Hepburn he'd come see her performance, of which she was proud. On the way to the airport in California, Tracy, who hated to fly, changed his mind and simply never showed up.

For all Hepburn's bold remarks about never wanting children, she had one anyway. But unlike a genuine child, who eventually turns fifteen and wants nothing to do with you, Tracy demanded Hepburn's attention until the end of his days. She brushed off the astonishing inequity of the entire arrangement by proclaiming, "Love has nothing to do with what you are expecting to get—only with what you are expecting to give—which is everything." Even Hallmark would steer clear of that one.

——◆——

I see I've drawn a relationship that we in our times might characterize as dysfunctional. Codependency, defined as "of or pertaining to a relationship in which one person is physically or psychologically addicted, as to alcohol or gambling, and the other person is psychologically dependent on the first in an unhealthy way," didn't enter the vernacular until 1985. I say this as an aside. It's safe to say Hepburn wouldn't have given a damn.

For the woman had a serious jones for redheaded tipplers, brooding, enigmatic men of Irish descent who hid their true natures with the help of Irish whiskey. Before Spencer Tracy, Hepburn developed a deep and devoted attachment to John Ford (*Grapes of Wrath*, *The Searchers*), who directed her in *Mary of Scotland*. Hepburn and "Sean," as she called him, may have become lovers, but Ford was married (albeit miserably) and would never be party to the sort of modern arrangement Hepburn struck with Tracy.

We all have our perverse attractions. A college friend has more or less squandered her life marrying one greaser/poet after the next. She won't listen to reason, that there is only one genuine greaser/poet in the land, and his name is Bruce Springsteen. He is currently unavailable, and too short for her. Another friend keeps getting entangled with laconic, meat-and-potatoes men generally thought by one and all to be beneath her station. I'm sure it's more complicated than this, but she swears she developed a yen for such men by watching Tracy and Hepburn make it work in all their movies.

At any rate, Dr. Phil would certainly not approve of the Tracy/Hepburn dynamic. Can't you just see the two of them sitting on the set, shoulder to shoulder in their bucket chairs? Dr. Phil would tell Hepburn to get real. He would challenge her: "Kate! Why are you always rescuing this man!" He would tell her that he needed to get clean and sober on his own, that she could not do it for him. He would tell her that while she couldn't hope to control Spencer's behavior, she could take concrete steps to affair-proof her pseudomarriage. He would tell her to make goals for the relationship (stop carrying the man's luggage, for God's sake). Dr. Phil would never get this far, of course. Hepburn would tell him to mind his own damn business and hurl a shoe at his head.

But it begs the question, aside from physical attraction and chemistry, which reliably wanes as the vexations wax: what compelled Hepburn to not simply stay with Tracy, but to dedicate every ounce of her life to him? Especially since, as people like to point out, he would never be able to marry her. (Which, as we've seen, may have been fine with Hepburn. It's been said that Louise cherished the social benefits of being Mrs. Tracy, but had no sense of humor when it came to ministering to her husband's endless needs. Hepburn, for her part, enjoyed taking care of Tracy, but could leave anytime she felt the itch without suffering much in the way of self-recrimination, or the censure of her fans. She was, after all, the secret mistress; she wasn't expected to stay home and wash his socks. The whole situation was very European. We frown upon such a thing these days, but it seemed to work out for everyone concerned.)

Hepburn's many excellent biographers have struggled mightily to dissect and psychoanalyze Hepburn's near mystical devotion to the ever-grumpy, unappreciative Tracy, without much success. Hepburn herself said, "People are shocked that I gave up so much for a man. But you have to understand it gave me pleasure to make him happy, to ease his agony." Why would such a thing give Hepburn pleasure, when there were few other pleasant aspects to the relationship? Director Elia Kazan offered as good an explanation as anyone else: "The cause Kate believed in was Spencer."

The correct position to take regarding the love of someone

else's life is to defer to the Mystery of Love and Attachment. Unfortunately, biographers are not generally in a position to say, regarding their subject's love life, "Who the hell *knows* what she/he saw in her/him/them." There is simply no explaining the Mystery of Love and Attachment. There's just no knowing whom we're going to be willing to sleep on the floor for (my personal measure of devotion, which also includes camping). The question why we love whom we love remains unanswerable, now and forever an unholy mélange of who raised us, how they raised us, the values of the culture at the time in which we were born and raised, how our future beloved looked and smelled on the day we met, when and how we met, and finally, our own arbitrary decision to yoke ourselves to one person and not another. There are probably more variables, but you get the point.

Some biographers take the traditional Freudian route and say Tracy reminded Hepburn of her emotionally distant father. Women love men like their fathers: most of us have heard this truism from our mothers or our Psychology 101 professors. I believe that several country-western songs address the phenomenon as well. It sounds good, but to the best of our knowledge, Hep wasn't a drinker. Nor was he full of Irish malaise and whimsy. He was however, tight-lipped, remote, and judgmental, like Tracy. If Hepburn was attracted to men who allowed her to re-create her relationship with her father, they were the tragic-poet version of Hep—men so nervous and artistic, they had to throw up walls to defend themselves, erected with the aid of of booze.

The obvious alternate theory was that Hepburn was not mar-

rying her father, but attempting to emulate her brilliant, opinionated, passionate, but ultimately dutiful mother. In some ways Hepburn was no different from the rest of us; the imposing shadow of
Kit loomed over her. If she, Hepburn, could love a difficult man as
fully as her mother loved her father, then it would prove her worth
as a female. Tracy stimulated Hepburn's inner need to care for a
male authority figure. He spoke to her inner caretaker, which was
able to sniff out Tracy's ability to let her do everything. In this way
Tracy's and Hepburn's neuroses fit together like a pair of tight puz-
zle pieces. She insisted on doing everything for him, and he was
happy to let her do it. Still, Hepburn was nothing if not complicated: she loved doting on Tracy the way Kit doted on Hep, but
she was not about to be chained to the tea table at five, pretty and
fresh and ready to serve. Tracy's already married status allowed her
to have it both ways.

WHY WE LOVE WHOM WE LOVE,
SOME HALF-BAKED THEORIES

1. *You Reach a Certain Age and You Just Get Sick of Yourself*
Hepburn had been paddling her canoe, alone, for all those years.
Her independence and self-involvement were legendary. Her career
was the commander in chief of her existence. Tracy lumbered into
her life and rescued her from herself. It's a little-known secret:
sometimes accomplished women just want a break from their own
nature. After all, men traditionally have women to prop them up,
and women have only themselves. We get exhausted, year in, year

out, doing the same thing Fred Astaire did, only backward and in high heels.

2. Frank Zappa Was Right: The Older We Get the More Life Is Like High School

It's possible that for some deep-seated Jungian reason all women secretly long to hook up with the star of the football team (which Tracy was during his heyday). It's also possible that self-determination grows old. In high school the parameters of our lives were drawn by our parents. We couldn't hang out because we had to mow the lawn. We couldn't go to a party because our unreasonable mom said no. After Hepburn met Tracy, she began fashioning her career decisions around his needs and his schedule. We humans are pack animals. Maybe at the end of the day, it's just a plain old relief to have someone else's welfare on whom to base your decisions.

3. You Make Me Look Good

A strange thing happened after Hepburn made Tracy her reason for living: people liked her better. She seemed less self-absorbed, more human, more *humane*. Her acting got better, deeper, more nuanced. Could it be that all that luggage carrying and racing off to the Caribbean to find him comfy lodgings made her a better person? "Here's what's most important about Katharine Hepburn: not her career and not her brilliance and not her talent—it was her profound, unconditional love for Spencer Tracy. That was her greatest achievement," said Michael Moriarty, who costarred with Hepburn in *The Glass Menagerie*. It's a little over-the-top, but the point is well taken.

One of the greatest things Spencer Tracy ever did for Katharine Hepburn—perhaps the only thing he ever did for her—was show the world Hepburn could be brought in line, thus making her image and movies safe for public consumption.

4. Newton's Third Law of Motion, Applied to the Human Heart

"For every action, there is an equal and opposite reaction." To wit, every time you make a decision about love with your head, your heart becomes more eager to do something ill-advised, like run off with a rodeo clown.

Hepburn divorced Luddy without a care. Then she took up with a number of powerful men without missing a beat, or even her six A.M. tennis lesson at the Beverly Hills Hotel. Maybe some unsatisfied life force urged her to make Tracy her life's work because she'd been so clearheaded in her previous relationships. Maybe her life with Tracy would have been more balanced had she lost her head over some unworthy brute in her twenties, or better yet, her teens. Whatever else Tracy was, he was high maintenance, and there's only room for one high-maintenance person in a relationship. If you want that person to be *you*, best to allow the heart to have its way when you're young.

5. The Kick in the Head Phenomenon

I don't mean to harp on the luggage, but once when Hepburn was carrying Tracy's bags out of a popular hotel where they'd been staying in their customary separate suites, she saw fans and reporters waiting for them outside. She said, "Spence, don't make me do this, please." He said, "Don't worry, I'll fix it." Then he walked out ahead of her with a fake limp.

◆—◆

At the risk again of sounding like my mother, who believed that everything difficult and taxing in life had the power to "make you a better person," Hepburn's years with Tracy enriched her life and may have made her a better actress.

In each of the four films Hepburn made during the last decade of Tracy's life, she was nominated for or won an Oscar: *Suddenly, Last Summer* (1959); *Long Day's Journey into Night* (1962); *Guess Who's Coming to Dinner* (1967); and *The Lion in Winter* (1968).

Hepburn turned in her inspired, raucous, bittersweet performance as Eleanor of Aquitaine in *The Lion in Winter* a scant year after Tracy died. The imperious, witty, well-born Eleanor was a role well within Hepburn's range; still, Kate's nuanced performance as the aging, discarded matriarch was both hilarious and heartbreaking. Of her devastating portrayal, the *New York Times* said, "In the moments of deepest anguish she is vibrant with hot and tragic truth, an eloquent representation of a lovely woman brought to feeble, helpless ruin."

Empathy was never Hepburn's strong suit. But Tracy was simply and endlessly tragic. He was an alcoholic. A cold swim and serving of stewed fruit couldn't fix him. Hepburn's decades of devotion had apparently performed that which the drunken night swim was supposed to do for Tracy Lord in *The Philadelphia Story*—softened her up and made her human.

7

SOME THOUGHTS ON DENIAL

Hepburn Denies Denial; The Making of The African Queen *and the Death of Kit; Minimizing; Hepburn as Alarm Clock; It's the Material That's Upsetting; Some Thoughts on Therapy: A Useful Quiz*

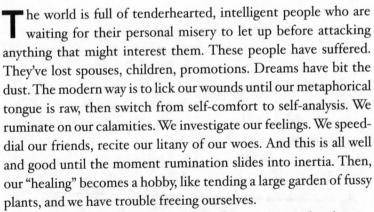

The world is full of tenderhearted, intelligent people who are waiting for their personal misery to let up before attacking anything that might interest them. These people have suffered. They've lost spouses, children, promotions. Dreams have bit the dust. The modern way is to lick our wounds until our metaphorical tongue is raw, then switch from self-comfort to self-analysis. We ruminate on our calamities. We investigate our feelings. We speed-dial our friends, recite our litany of our woes. And this is all well and good until the moment rumination slides into inertia. Then, our "healing" becomes a hobby, like tending a large garden of fussy plants, and we have trouble freeing ourselves.

Hepburn never had this problem because she refused to acknowledge she had problems. Despair and suffering were things on which other, less sensible people wasted valuable time. Loss was a fact of life, like gravity and the need to stay hydrated. Every problem could be solved by a swim in frigid water or a brisk walk. Catastrophes that would stop most people in their tracks were simply roadblocks for which an alternative route could be found. Pangs of remorse, regret, longing? Didn't have 'em. Pangs? "Not in my nature to pang," she'd say with conviction.

Even though Hepburn was born a hundred years ago, at a time when bucking up was the accepted method of coping, she was still a marvel of soldiering on. Navel-gazing, in her book, was self-indulgent and thus almost criminal. You would be hard-pressed to find someone, living or dead, who was less introspective. Even General Patton kept a diary. (He also believed in reincarnation.) Carrying on with aplomb in the face of life's setbacks was Kate's true métier, the thing at which she never failed to excel until her own death on June 29, 2003, when natural causes finally overwhelmed her resolve to pretend that everything was ducky.

To press on the way she did, you have to be practiced in the old, unfashionable art of denial. Hepburn was raised in the tradition. Both sides of the family included men who had suffered from depression and had eventually offed themselves. While the Hepburns shocked their genteel Hartford neighbors with dinner-table discussions of birth control and venereal disease, the names of their forebears who committed suicide were never mentioned, as if they'd never even been born. Likewise, after Hepburn's older brother, Tom, was found hanging, his name was never uttered again.

In defense of what must seem pathologically repressive in

these cozy times of sharing and caring, we must remember that at the turn of the last century, when Kit and Hep came of age, no one talked about suicide. The shame itself was worse than that of having a known adulterer in the family. Suicide was believed to be caused by a hereditary madness, and in any case, there was nothing to be done aside from avoiding cultivating a nervous temperament. Pretending the situation didn't exist was clearly the best solution.

◆—◆—◆

Hepburn's gift for pressing ever on could be witnessed in the spring of 1951, when, at the age of forty-four, she was scheduled to set out for the Belgian Congo (now the Democratic Republic of the Congo) to shoot *The African Queen*, which Hepburn had agreed to because it was going to be shot on location in Africa, and not on the studio soundstage. Shooting on location in a foreign country was an exotic proposition in 1951. Just getting to Africa meant sailing first to England. Regular transatlantic jet travel was still a thing of the future (as were movie stars commandeering entire African resorts for the purpose of giving birth to their affluent, American child).

John Huston, the movie's director and a somewhat obsessive lunatic, crisscrossed Africa by plane, racking up about twenty-five thousand miles, before settling on the Ruiki River for his production, smack in the heart of darkness. The shoot was one long slog through leech-infested mud. Cast and crew battled hornets, blood flukes, and army ants and fled from the poisonous green mambas, which set up camp in the outhouse, all while enduring bouts of malaria and dysentery, which both Humphrey Bogart and Huston avoided by engaging in a self-prescribed regime of near alcohol poisoning. Kate stuck to water and got sicker than anyone. On the "set"—a clearing where they dropped the equipment—there were no dressing rooms. There weren't even any chairs. There was a mirror, which Kate took it upon herself to lug from location to location. When it broke, she lugged along the pieces. At night, huge moths flew into the dining tent, knocked themselves out on the overhead lights, then dropped straight onto the plates.

But this adventure was yet to come.

Prior, on St. Patrick's Day of 1951, the morning after the closing night of the Theater Guild's Broadway production of *As You Like It* (Kate and her tennis-toned legs played Rosalind), Kate was at home in Hartford with Mother and Dad.

Since the topic of this chapter is denial, this is as good a time as any to mention the unwavering esteem in which Hepburn held her parents. Like Spencer Tracy, they could do no wrong. They were never annoying, insensitive, pigheaded, unfair, moody, or just plain wrong. Granted, Hepburn came of age long before James Dean rebelled without a cause, but you would still be hard-pressed to find another grown woman who was so universally approving of mom and dad. Throughout her life she was unwavering in her adoration. They were fascinating. They were heroic. They were, not to repeat myself—but Kate did, whenever their names were mentioned, so why not—perfect and wonderful.

Spending a lifetime in unconditional appreciation of your parents is tremendously expedient, if you can pull it off. Mark Twain said, "When I was a boy of fourteen, my father was so ignorant I could hardly stand to have the old man around. But when I got to be twenty-one, I was astonished at how much he'd learned in seven years."

Most us fall in the Twain camp and not the Hepburn camp. We lumber through stages in which we worship and glorify our parents, question their wisdom, think they're pure idiots, find ourselves irritated by their annoying insistence on breathing in and out, find ourselves even *more* irritated when it turns out they're not so stupid after all, and finally come to accept that not only are we just like them, we rather love them after all. We waste untold hours in bars and on the phone kvetching to our friends about how impossible they are. To take the position that they're perfect and fascinating would save so much time.

Hepburn spent that happy morning chatting with Kit about her performance in *As You Like It*, which must have been a heady experience for Kate, since Mother was a serious person, with serious tastes, and thought her daughter's movies were pure dross, her movie-queen fame a little tacky, and that that Spencer Tracy person she'd brought around once, only once, was deeply uninteresting. But now that Kate had begun to master Shakespeare—that was something altogether different. That was a glorious achievement.

In the afternoon Kate went for a walk with Hep, returning in time for tea. Hep is said to have supported his wife in all her radical, neighbor-shocking political activities, so long as she was at her post behind the tea cart every day at five to serve up the scones and cucumber sandwiches. On this day, Kit wasn't there.

Kate found her mother in her dressing gown lying on her bed, the sheet pulled half over her. Her position suggested she'd been feeling faint, but she was dead. Kate only allowed her father into the room after she'd rearranged her mother's limbs and smoothed the sheets, staging the scene so it appeared as if Kit had perhaps passed during a satisfying nap, though given her marital history, and the activities she'd sacrificed for decades in order to be obediently behind the tea cart, it was obvious Kit would never have been lollygagging in such a manner at teatime.

Hepburn phoned Tracy and told him the news, but said that he shouldn't disrupt the shooting schedule of his current film to come East. Tracy, who loathed flying, or tending to Hepburn in any way (Kate's life with Tracy was one long stint behind the tea cart), was happy to comply with her wishes.

Kit was cremated and buried in the family plot three days later.

A mere three weeks later Kate sailed to England and then on to the staggering hardship of making *The African Queen*. Few experiences provide the sort of closeness and camaraderie as does the making of a movie; yet throughout the arduous months of filming in the Belgian Congo, no one knew the star had just lost her mother. Years later Hepburn would see fit to write a memoir about the adventure, *The Making of "The African Queen," or, How I Went to Africa with Bogart, Bacall and Huston and Almost Lost My Mind*; in it, Kit's unexpected death is mentioned only in passing.

◆–◆

Denial is defined loosely as "refusing to perceive the more unpleasant aspects of an external reality." As defined and conceptualized
by Anna Freud, it is at the top of the list of defense mechanisms.*
Denial is one of those topics, like lawyers, that can hardly be mentioned nowadays without an accompanying punch line. We live in
such perpetual fear of being in the dreaded pathological state of
denial that we question even our most benign assertions. A friend
asks how we're doing. We say, "Fine," which prompts the inner us
to say, "Really? Fine? *Fine?* Who are you kidding? Your quarterly
taxes are due next week, and what about that strange sore on the
back of your calf? You're not fine. You're far from fine. To say 'Fine'
is not to face the troubling reality of your true situation. You're in
denial is what you are."

Kate was an avid practitioner of the form of denial known as
minimizing. She was able to pretend that the death of her mother
was simply "part of life," something to be accepted without any of
that time-consuming grieving. The conundrum, of course, is that
death and loss are both a part of life *and* devastating events.

The African Queen finished shooting in Léopoldville in July. The
entire company repaired to London for six more weeks of additional filming. Hepburn was still plagued by dysentery and had lost
twenty pounds. In London an internist was called in to see if anything could be done, and she was made well enough to finish the

---

*Other popular defense mechanisms include projection, regression, sublimation,
and intellectualization.

picture. When Hepburn arrived back in California in September to begin filming *Pat and Mike* with Spencer Tracy, she was still weak. During her absence Tracy had been drinking. He'd sunk into one of his black, Irish moods. *Pat and Mike* was the last movie Kate would do for MGM. Tracy didn't know what he was going to do next, didn't know what he *could* do next. Hepburn threw herself back into the demanding chore of shoring him up and drying him out.

Despite their individual offscreen hardships, *Pat and Mike* was one of the best of the Tracy/Hepburn offerings. Tracy stars as a grizzled sports promoter and Hepburn as a top lady athlete who's both a brilliant golfer and tennis player, but chokes every time her judgmental Ken-doll-like fiancé shows up to watch her perform. Perhaps it's because both stars were crawling from their particular wreckage that it's more low-key than their other comedies, both breezy and brilliant.

In February 1952, Hepburn was off again, sailing to London to star in George Bernard Shaw's *The Millionairess*. In the mind of Hepburn's late mother, the sun rose and set on the genius of Shaw. No matter whether Kate was running on fumes after *Pat and Mike* wrapped, she was determined to go to London to play the glamorous, bossy Epifania. *The Millionairess* is one of Shaw's lesser plays, but Shaw was Shaw, and Hepburn was going to give it all she had.

Since the death of Kit a year earlier, Hepburn had filmed two movies on two different continents. She'd contracted a near fatal disease. She'd discovered shortly after her mother was buried that her father had burned all of Kit's diaries, letters, and papers, documents that contained not only the essence of the beloved Kit and a lot of Hepburn family history, but also the story of the fight for women's suffrage in the form of Kit's correspondence with Margaret Sanger and Emmeline Pankhurst. Hep couldn't have cared less. The past was the past, burn the stuff and be on with it. With even more expedience he married one of his nurses. Hepburn's brothers and sisters expressed varying degrees of outrage, but Hepburn refused to say a word against him. Meanwhile, Tracy showed up in London to film scenes for *The Plymouth Adventure*, his new girlfriend, Gene Tierney, in tow.

Hepburn played Epifania at the pitch of a toddler in mid-temper-tantrum. From the moment she strode onstage the volume knob was on ten. Barbara Leaming, in her 1995 biography, described it thus: "Kate hopped up and down; whooped with delight; descended a staircase three steps at a time; did a swan dive onto her face." Hepburn ranted. Hepburn hurled props. Broke chairs. Knocked down her costars. Spat in their faces. Howled and raged. The consensus among her friends was that she was confusing a public nervous breakdown with acting.

In London, the critics loved her, believing she was epitome of the wacky American. When *The Millionairess* moved to New York, the reviews were lukewarm. All that hysteria was less amusing to an indigenous audience. Walter Kerr, writing about Hepburn's performance for the *New York Herald Tribune*, said, "Katharine Hepburn is beautiful, radiant, vital, and not very good. At times, she sounds like an alarm clock that no one can shut off."

Epifania says in the play, "What is life if not lived in the deep end?" which sounds terrifically romantic and daring, unless, of course, you actually find yourself in the deep end. One day near the end of the London run Hepburn collapsed with fever. She lost her voice. To the fans who hounded her, she was monstrous, consenting to sign someone's autograph book, then tearing out the pages and ripping them to shreds there on the street.

Even though Hepburn was incapable of actually sitting down and grieving, she could have done with a bit of a rest. She needed to fold up her tent and disappear into the desert for a while, but she couldn't do it. She was like a shark, whose only evolutionary flaw is the inability to swim backward. Ever forward she went, habitually and compulsively, denying anything was wrong. But striding on only works for so long, even for a near superhero like Hepburn.

◆—◆—◆

I would be in denial myself if I didn't admit that it heartens me to see this glimpse of Hepburn's ordinariness. No one gets away without grieving the death of her mother. It's like Christmas. You can spend it in Mozambique or sit in your apartment and watch the Sci-Fi Channel movie marathon as if it's any other time of the year, but sometime on December 25 you *know* what day it is. Childhood memories of better times seep up from some deep brain wrinkle, and you become nostalgic or sad or regretful.

It's reassuring to hear that Hepburn could not keep everything going indefinitely—the film career, the bicontinental theater career, the round-the-clock Tracy-tending, the six A.M. tennis lessons, the golf games, the crack-of-dawn swims (on the mornings of her tennis lessons, did she also swim?), the avid letter-writing, the traveling, the script-reading on behalf of both her and Tracy, and everything else.

Even those of us who adore Hepburn find something insufferable about her on occasion. Failure could not slow her down. The dysentery aside, she never seemed to get sick. She seemed to have escaped menstruation and menopause entirely. Did a day ever dawn when she could simply not get out of her bathrobe?

There is something to be said for a little wallowing, a little self-pity, a little wondering why me and not the other guy. Or, if you were as fortunate as Hepburn always claimed to be, there is the occasional bout of existential malaise that pesters like a mosquito bite. There is sitting with your feet on the coffee table pondering the hole in the toe of your sock, wondering why everything must pass, why people die, why we clean the house when it will only get dirty again.

No one can escape it.

For the problem with ignoring grief is that it doesn't go away. It's not a harmless rash. Whoever said that time heals all needed to have his head examined. Primo Levi said that sometimes an injury cannot be healed, that it extends through time. The writer Jonathan Safran Foer wondered recently, "What if time *is* the wound?"

The sock-hole-pondering is without a doubt a waste of time. While you are wallowing, someone else is at hot yoga, putting in extra hours at work, or writing her novel. But there is no skipping the wallowing, the pondering, the reliving, and the reassessing. You can't just make up your mind not to partake of basic human misery. It's like stuffing a golf bag into a full-to-bursting coat closet.

It's fine until you need a jacket, then you open the door and wind up breaking a toe.

•—•—•

In 1959 Hepburn endured what she often claimed was her worst film acting experience in her life. She played Violet Venable, one of Tennessee Williams's demented mothers, in the mucid and overwrought *Suddenly, Last Summer*. The ruined son, Sebastian, a failed poet and sadistic lover of young boys, is murdered on a beach in Spain in a way that has made Mrs. Venable's niece, Catherine (Elizabeth Taylor), go "mad." To prevent Catherine's episodes of insanity, Mrs. Venable wants her to have a lobotomy, but the real reason Mrs. Venable wants to lobotomize her niece is because she knows the truth about Sebastian's sexual orientation and his shocking demise.

Kate protested with great schoolmarm self-righteousness that the material was simply offensive. Sebastian's murder was an act of cannibalism; he was eaten right there on the beach in midday by street urchins.

It's more likely that what truly rankled Hepburn was the matter at the core of the film: her own character's obsession with hiding the truth of her son's death. Had Kate given any thought to the deeper implications of what it would mean to play Violet Venable, she might have thought to herself, "Hmmm—too close to home—not for me."

Instead, Kate kept wanting to play the dowager Venable as a madwoman—for who but a madwoman would go to such lengths to hide the truth? But Violet wasn't insane, just distraught and controlling. Hepburn and director Joseph Mankiewicz argued about her performance every day. Hepburn simply couldn't bear the thought that someone who was not completely around the bend might be capable of going to extremes to hide the truth about a boy's death, someone such as, well, her own mother or dad. Allowing this association to creep into her mind was not good, not comforting. Very anxiety-making, actually. Kate kept trying to arm wrestle Mrs. Venable into lunacy; Mankiewicz kept a firm grip on the situation. At the end of filming, so appalled and disgusted was she, Hepburn marched up to him and spat on the floor in front of him. They call that acting out, not acting.

A successful course of therapy would have helped Hepburn get over her loss, but she thought it was all a load of bull, pure hokum. When her friend and future memoirist A. Scott Berg confessed to her that he meditated, she scoffed in his face. Hepburn subscribed to the theory that work cured whatever ailed you, and since you were going to recover from your loss anyway, you might as well just skip to the all-better part and be done with it.

—◆—

All this said, one must acknowledge that since Hepburn's day society has overcorrected itself. Now, we are so afraid of being in denial, we live in perpetual devastation over the death of our first dog. Once, I had a student who could not come to class for several days because her daughter's hamster had died. We are hyperaware of every wrong done to us; we worry that whatever it is we're angry about, perhaps we are really angry about something else. We would be well served to fold a bit of Hepburnian-style denial into our lives. If leggings can come back into style, so can bucking up.

Therapy helps us find and name our particular demons, but does it exorcise them? Or, does it serve mostly to put us on speaking terms with our troubles, but doesn't help solve them? Furthermore, do we want to be quote-unquote cured? Is therapy like an over-the-counter painkiller that merely takes the edge off, enough so we can trudge along, free of agony, but fails to inspire us to do much of anything, other than enjoy what life sees fit to put in our way? There's every reason to believe we'll never solve all our problems. Is it unreasonable to imagine we might allow ourselves to be driven by our unanswered questions, our unresolved situations?

Hepburn may dimly have been aware of this. In one interview she said she thought when an actor was miserable, he did his best work: "So most actors I think, fundamentally, can use the miseries. I think that any kind of an artist generally can use the sorrows and the miseries for creative effect."

A quick survey of many of the world's great artists does seem to indicate that a certain amount of misery breeds achievement. Émile Zola, the prolific French writer, turned out one memorable novel after another until middle age, when he fell deeply in love for the first time and the quality of his work went straight downhill. The happy man is the enemy of progress after all.

Would Kate have done more or better work if she weren't driven by her specific demons? Would years of analysis have made her a better person, a better actress, a better artist? She holds the record for most Best Actress nominations (twelve), most wins (four), and longest span between her first Oscar and her last. Oscars are subjective, of course. Film historians and critics believe Hepburn didn't deserve to win for *Guess Who's Coming to Dinner* and should have won for *The Philadelphia Story* and *The African Queen*. Would she have made fewer great movies if she hadn't been a believer in denial?

For better or worse Hepburn possessed a great gift for simply putting things out of her mind, a lost art that would serve us modern overanalyzers well. She famously lived in the moment. Before Nike made the slogan famous, Hepburn just did it. The key to always and endlessly just doing it, to stoically soldiering onward, is living in a certain amount of denial.

TEST *YOUR* ABILITY TO MAKE DENIAL WORK FOR YOU

1. You find out your husband is having an affair with your best friend on the day before you're scheduled to take the bar exam. Do you:

a) Focus on your doing the best you can on the exam, then confront him afterward.

b) Smother your husband with a pillow the night before.

c) Sob all the way to the exam, thereby ensuring your eyes

will be too puffy to read the questions, thus assuring your failure.

d) Say, Huh? No way. Not only am I way hotter than my friend, very soon I'm going to be pulling down six figures as a hot-shot defense attorney.

2. You're a thirty-seven-year-old professional figure skater who is so winded you cannot complete the short program. Everyone says you're finished, including your coach, who no longer wants to work with you. Your response is:

a) Allow some time to pass, during which you reassess your current fitness level and future ice-skating goals.

b) Think: I need a new costume. No one can do decent work with that kind of wedgie.

c) Blame it on the ice.

d) Tell everyone you're so glad that pathetic loser dumped you, relieving you of the chore of dumping him. With such lousy coaching, how on earth are you supposed to make the Olympic team, anyway?

3. You are putting away your son's clean socks and find a sandwich baggie full of what appears to be oregano in his underwear drawer. Do you:

a) Tell him you were putting away his laundry and found his stash, listen to his explanation before gently reminding him to just say no to drugs.

b) Form a prayer circle.

c) Slam the drawer shut, run out of the room, stuff the clean
   socks back in the laundry hamper and let someone else
   deal with it.

d) Commend your son for taking his cooking class so seriously.

4. The guy you had a lovely date with two Fridays ago hasn't
   called. You think:

a) He's just not that into me.

b) He mentioned he was thinking of getting a new cell. It's
   probably not activated yet.

c) His mother's probably in town and he's consumed with
   entertaining her.

d) He's just afraid of his feelings of deep and abiding love for me.

5. You find a lump. You think:

a) Even if it is cancer, the disease is quite treatable in its early
   stages, and there's every reason to believe I'll recover.

b) It could just be a cyst. I won't know anything until I see the
   doctor.

c) It's just a cyst.

d) Lump? What lump?

6. Your married lover won't leave his wife. You think:

a) Fine, I've had enough, it's over. I'm worth more than this.

b) Just wait until I send her those racy e-mails.

c) I'll smother her with a pillow.

d) Who wants to get married anyway?

7. You've been wearing the same hairstyle for so long your stylist gives you the Liza Minnelli Alert (i.e., you need a change). Do you:

a) Thank your stylist for being frank with you and ask her to give you a new look.

b) Run out of the salon in tears and find another hair stylist.

c) Tell your stylist she's confusing you with someone else, and that you've actually only worn your hair this way for a short time (cut the actual number of decades in half.)

d) Laugh uproariously and say, "Actually, Liza Minnelli's hairdresser keeps telling Liza that she's turning into me."

8. You back out of your driveway and run over the neighbor. He will live, but will need to have a plate put in his head. Do you:

a) Apologize to his family and offer to pay his medical bills.

b) Send over a casserole.

c) Insist that he leaped behind your car—clearly indicative of a suicide wish.

d) Wonder what the fuss is about. You know many people with plates in their head. Not only have they adapted quite well, they can now stick refrigerator magnets to their foreheads and are the life of every party.

9. Your mother-in-law found your bottle. You say:

a) I confess, I have a terrible drinking problem and I'm going to seek help today.

b) Weep and promise to change, then smother her with a pillow.

c) What's she got her panties in a twist about? At least you only have one hiding place.

d) I've never seen it before in my life, it must belong to your son.

SCORING:
1 point for every a
2 points for every b
3 points for every c
4 points for every d

36 points: Hepburnian Stoic

9–35 points: Hopeless Sniveler

8

FEAR MANAGEMENT, THE
HEPBURN WAY

*Hepburn Was Generally Not Afraid, Except When She Was Terrified; Hepburn,
High-Sensation Seeker; A Nervous Hepburn Is Caught by a Hidden Camera;
Brooks Atkinson Is Not a Fan; Finding a Mentor; Finding Courage*

Hepburn earned a reputation over the years for fearlessness, but people who knew her well claimed she was quite shy, and much of the time quite afraid. This makes sense if we think about Picasso, who painted every single day because every single day he needed to prove he was worth something, if only to himself. We assume great people are great on account of some natural superiority, but it may be their fears (of not measuring up, of failing, of mediocrity) that continue to drive them long after the less fearful among us have settled into our Barcalounger, more or less content with our lot and our TiVo.

In her later years Hepburn admitted she'd spent her entire life being afraid, that "it terrifies anyone who is intelligent to do anything," that the whole human race is, at any given time, petrified, and that "fear is something we all suffer from."

Did she seriously believe this about herself, or was this sweeping generalization meant to fend off having to parse her actions or account for her motivations, a favorite Hepburn trick?

Even now, it seems impossible to take her words at face value. Even since Hepburn was a wee thing growing up in Hartford, she routinely cultivated activities that would give most of us a case of night terrors.

ACTIVITIES HEPBURN ENJOYED, BUT WOULD GIVE THE REST OF US PAUSE

1. Breaking and entering. Hepburn was a self-proclaimed gifted second-story man. She told an apocryphal story about how once she entered via a third-floor skylight and nearly plunged to her death. Somehow, she managed to save herself from falling. Images of Tom Cruise in the original *Mission: Impossible* come to mind. The only thing she ever stole was a nutcracker shaped like a crocodile; guilt got the best of her and she snuck back into the house to return it.

2. Flying. During her early years in Hollywood, Hepburn thought nothing of zipping back and forth across the country with Leland Hayward and Howard Hughes. Modern aviation was—well, there was no sense that there would be such a thing as "modern aviation." It was still too early to tell whether this airplane-flying business was going to stick, or whether it would

forever remain a curiosity, like hot-air balloons. Both jet travel and the Federal Aviation Administration, which was established to help prevent the increasingly common midair collisions, were decades in the future.

3. Travel to far-flung locales. Hepburn loved to travel at a time when just getting to Europe meant enduring an ocean crossing and the possible thrill of two straight weeks of seasickness. She set out without having a clue what she would find when she arrived; in our times this sort of haphazard method of going warrants its own television show. She did *The African Queen* so she could see Africa and signed on with the Old Vic Theater to perform a trio of Shakespeare plays in order to see Australia.

4. Ocean swims. The average temperature in Long Island Sound in January is thirty-four degrees Fahrenheit. Whenever Hepburn was at Fenwick, whatever the season, she took a morning swim. The thought of hypothermia or being swept out to sea apparently never occurred to her. It is unlikely Hepburn thought much about the risk of shark attack.

5. Hurricane watching. During the hurricane that destroyed the first Fenwick house in 1938, she seemed relatively unconcerned when the trees were flattened by the wind. Submitting to evacuation would mean missing all the excitement.

6. Driving in Manhattan during rush hour. Hepburn felt this
   was a great unsung sport.

––•––

During the last half of the last century scientists began studying
this sort of behavior. If anyone could have convinced Hepburn
to sit still for a few psychological tests, she, and they, would have
found that she was a High-Sensation Seeker, a term coined by a ge-
neticist named Marvin Zuckerman, who has made a study of people like Evel Knievel, who would rather jump a motorcycle over a
twenty-foot-long box of rattlesnakes than read a book. Hepburn
and her ilk share common personality traits: they're high achiev-
ers, unsentimental, independent, and self-sufficient. They're creative extroverts who get bored easily, are excited by novelty, and
tend to like a variety of sexual partners, vacation destinations, and
food. At a Turkish restaurant they're the ones who order the sheep
eyes. Unless, like Hepburn, they wouldn't be caught dead in a
restaurant.

––•––

Despite her high-sensation-seeking personality, we can take Hepburn at her word on one point: she did possess a lifelong case
of stage fright. Evidence to support this exists in the form of Hepburn's unprecedented appearance on *The Dick Cavett Show* in Oc-
tober of 1973.

The Dick Cavett Show ran opposite Johnny Carson and was considered the thinking person's late-night television show. Basically, Cavett just sat and talked to people. Unlike Carson, he invited rock stars to sit down and have a word, rather than simply provide the occasional musical interlude. He chatted with Jimi Hendrix, David Bowie, and the Jefferson Airplane. He devoted entire ninety-minute shows to conversations with Alfred Hitchcock, Orson Welles, Fred Astaire, and, over two nights, Katharine Hepburn.

When Hepburn agreed to appear on the Cavett show, she had never done television. She was sixty-six years old, although at the time her actual birthday was still a mystery. Before the interview, she asked to be allowed to familiarize herself with the set, meet Cavett, and in general see what was what. On the day she showed up for her inspection, unbeknownst to her, the camera was rolling.

Out she comes in her customary uniform: white turtleneck, black overshirt, khakis, and wide-strapped sandals. Her hair was where her hair always was when she wasn't playing a role, on top of her head in a messy bun. She examines everything. She says the carpet is ugly and offers to bring a rug from home to cover it. She doesn't like the paint, has issues with the flimsy coffee table on which she will never in a million years be able to prop her feet. She quibbles without end, as if to pause would invite her to stop and think about what, exactly, she was doing. She asks about switching out the table, and when no one answers her immediately, she throws her hands up and cries, "Doesn't anybody ever listen?!" She tugs at her turtleneck. She obsesses about the flimsy table, eventually changing it with a taller one that sits between the two chairs. She is ornery, critical, imperious, and nervous. Watching her fuss, you can imagine all the different behaviors she engages in to stem her fear.

Finally, she settles into the chair, sticks her feet up on the table, and declares she wants to do the taping right then, with no makeup, no band, no audience. Cavett, dressed as if on his way to the marina, in white pants and white deck shoes, complies without missing a beat, as if a rare bird has perched on the edge of his backyard bird feeder and he daren't scare it off.

———◆———

Hepburn did not fear the camera. She realized early on that she photographed well and, in any case, was under no obligation to view the final results; she claimed never to have seen the final cut of most of her movies.

The theater was something else. Any bad stuff that was going to happen regarding her performance was going to happen right there and then. There was no second or third or twenty-third take if she messed up. She viewed the audience as her natural enemy. She believed they did not come to be entertained, but to sit in judgment.

When she'd decided to become an actress, she had not counted on having to manage two contradictory realities: yearning desperately to go onstage while being panic-stricken by it at the same time.

Opening nights were the worst. Once, before she left for Hollywood and her starring role in *A Bill of Divorcement*, she'd been hired as an understudy to the leading lady in *The Big Pond*. The play was previewing at the Great Neck Theater before heading to Broadway. As the story goes, to calm her nerves Hepburn went for a stroll in some nearby woods. There, like some scatterbrained fairy-tale character, she dined on berries and milk and took a nap. When she awoke, she realized it was late; she hurried back to the theater with ten minutes to spare.

Hepburn strode onstage that night in Great Neck, and when the audience chortled at her first line (in which she imitated the French accent of her husband), she lost her mind. She went from wondering how she could possibly *talk*, how she could possibly *walk*, how she could possibly even *move*, to thinking she was brilliant. Her voice got higher and faster, until no one could understand her, and her freckled complexion was so red with exertion and excitement, it looked as if she might explode, like a spring-loaded party popper. After the performance, she was fired.

Hepburn's stage fright was chronic, incurable. Before she went onstage she would suffer intestinal misery, her face would become blotchy, her entire body shook.

Hepburn never got used to making that first entrance. The older she got, the more the world accepted her as a serious actress, the more terrified she became. It worsened over the years, thus giving the lie to what we all tell our kids in an effort to comfort them: that things will get better when they get older. The flinty truth is that mostly things get worse, including our fears. Solace is found in acclimation: we may not overcome our terror, but we get used to the sensation of being terrified.

Hepburn even fretted over opening in *The Philadelphia Story*, her now legendary comeback vehicle. Even though the role of Tracy Lord fit Hepburn like a bespoke suit, and the play was well received in previews, Hepburn was worried about bringing the show to New York. She kept begging the producers to stay on the road, until they finally forced her to open on Broadway.

Hepburn's fear of Broadway was understandable. The esteemed Brooks Atkinson of the *New York Times*, considered the most important drama critic of the time, was no fan.

About Hepburn's awful turn in *The Lake* he said, "There is no point in pursuing Miss Hepburn with her limitations as a dramatic actress. The simple fact is that as a result of her sensational achievements on the screen she has been projected into a stage part that requires more versatility than she has had time to develop. She still needs considerable training, especially for a voice that has such an unpleasant timbre."

About her turn as Jane Eyre, while Atkinson was willing to admit that she was "an uncommonly interesting person," he still took issue with her acting abilities, at one point calling her monotonous.

Ouch.

This was most unnerving. Unlike Dorothy Parker, with her "Hepburn ran the gamut of emotions from A to B" quip, Atkinson wasn't a wiseass. His reviews were well regarded. His was the voice of reason. He never missed an opening night and never left his seat during intermission, to avoid being distracted by gossip. Hepburn imagined him waiting for her with narrowed eyes and a sharpened pencil.

What was she to do?

Why, pretend she wasn't even in New York, of course.

The Philadelphia Story had recently enjoyed a successful out-of-town run. When the company arrived in Manhattan, and the show was being readied to open at the Shubert, Hepburn focused on convincing herself she was in Indianapolis. She ignored her Turtle Bay town house and checked into a hotel, as if she were still on the road. She shut out the city by keeping her curtains drawn. On opening night, she strong-armed Joseph Cotten (in the Cary Grant role) and Van Heflin (in the Jimmy Stewart role) into toasting to their continued success in . . . Indianapolis.

Although Hepburn was still nervous, her ruse managed to help dial down the hysteria a notch.

Atkinson raved, "Certainly Mr. Barry has written Miss Hepburn's ideal part. It has whisked away the monotony and reserve that have kept her acting in the past within a very small compass. As the daughter of the rich she plays with grace, jauntiness and warmth—moving across the stage like one who is liberated from self-consciousness and taking a pleasure in acting that the audience can share."

The triumph of *The Philadelphia Story* was fairy-tale-like, and I wish I could report that Hepburn's Why, Yes, We *Are* Still in Kansas! (or Indiana) technique of calming her nerves was a magic bullet that cured her of stage fright once and for all and won the undying, unwavering admiration of her arch-nemesis.

Alas, three years later Hepburn was back on Broadway in Barry's *Without Love*, about which Atkinson harrumphed, "As the

unloved wife, Miss Hepburn is giving a mechanical performance
that is not without considerable gaucherie."

◆—◆

Fear of bees, of bacteria, of storms, of taking tests, and of vomiting.
Fear of needles, crossing bridges, doctors. Fear of thinking (people
suffering from phonemophobia are afraid of new thoughts, which,
by virtue of being new, are also unexpected). Public speaking is routinely listed as our greatest fear, but one list of common phobias puts
fear of spiders as number one. People are also afraid of heights, cancer, closed and open spaces. In the social arena, people fear success,
failure, being judged, being ignored, abandoned, rejected, embarrassed, and intimate. People are afraid of the numbers 13, 666, and,
strangely, 8. Some of the less common fears—but not so uncommon
that they lack proper names—are the fear of blushing, fear of ob-
jects set to the left side of the body, fear of moisture, wooden ob-
jects, and long waits. Consecotaleophobia is the fear of chopsticks.
Nowhere, on any of the long lists of human phobias, could I find fear
of attempting to become a Shakespearean actress in middle age.

Hepburn was forty-three when she decided to accept the role
of Rosalind, in the Theater Guild's production of *As You Like It*.
With 721 speaking lines, it's one of Shakespeare's heartiest female
roles, the ultimate test of an actress's range. It's also an ingénue role
(Vanessa Redgrave played Rosalind to great acclaim at age twenty-
four), a coming-of-age piece in which Rosalind and her buddy Celia

evolve from girls to women. In that any classical role could be said to be written for Hepburn, it might have been the cross-dressing Rosalind, who disguises herself as the witty young boy Ganymede and romps around the Forest of Arden with his "sister," the feminine, sensible Celia, cracking wise, speaking out, and acting up; still, in 1950, forty-three was not the cusp of middle age, it was not the verge of middle age, it was full-blown middle age. And the term *middle age* had not yet been reconceived as *midlife*, which sounds so bouncy and positive, like *midstride*, the ugly word *age* expunged completely from the concept of no longer being young.

Consider: the same year, Bette Davis, one year Hepburn's junior, starred in *All About Eve*, in which she embodied the aging actress Margo Channing. Aging is the key concept here. There was nothing bouncy and fresh-faced about Davis; she had been a woman for a long time; indeed, she was rapidly passing from womanhood into jaded cronehood, with a cigarette stuck to her lip, firing off one-liners that could give you a paper cut. The heroic workhorse Joan Crawford staged a career comeback in her fortieth year, starring in the frenzied melodrama *Mildred Pierce*.

It's doubtful Hepburn paid any attention to the cultural significance of her age. Indeed, only in her forties did she begin to take the art of acting seriously. Anyway, her own demons kept her plenty busy. She harbored the nagging suspicion that she was a personality and not a real actress. She knew she could play herself, but was that the *only* thing she could do? Over the years both theater and movie critics liked to point this out when she turned in a disastrous performance. In one disparaging review, the critic pointed out that

Hepburn "makes no attempt" to inhabit the role; "She is just Miss Hepburn, vivid, varying little, adored by a vast public."

➤—◆

Some of the basic demands of performing Shakespeare include:

> Massive amounts of memorization
> Learning the feel of the old words in your mouth
> Grappling with the meaning of what you're actually going on about
> Discovering how best to inhabit an unfamiliar sort of character
> Learning to inhabit the words and not simply recite them
> Making the character's situation and concerns resonate with contemporary audiences
> Mastering the transitions between emotional states without resorting to melodrama
> What in the hell am I talking about again?
> The athletic demands
> The weight of four hundred years of production history

➤—◆

Hepburn was in superb physical condition from a lifetime of swimming, golfing, and tennis playing. Still, in the summer of 1949, she went to New York to begin training for her own personal marathon, leaving Tracy to mope in California. Rehearsals for *As You Like It* would begin in the fall, and Hepburn prepared herself for her upcoming challenge by jogging every morning in Central Park. She was already tough, and her good idea for combating her fear was to get tougher.

Getting tougher also included finding a mentor.

Born in 1878, Constance Collier was a classically trained British actress weaned on Shakespeare. At age three she played Fairy Peasblossom in a production of *A Midsummer Night's Dream*. In 1906, at age twenty-eight, she played Cleopatra in *Antony and Cleopatra*. Square of jaw, strong of brow, with enormous dark eyes and a head of wild curls, she was striking, and strikingly tall.

Hepburn and Collier met during the filming of *Stage Door*, in which Collier played Catherine Luther, the dotty old acting coach who despite her decrepitude still lives at the Footlights Club—a misfit among all that striving, uninformed youth—and insists on the importance of knowing the classics. Hepburn's Terry Randall—who's snubbed for her wealth and "breeding"—shares Luther's devotion to Shakespeare, as demonstrated by this exchange:

CATHERINE: I can't tell you how interested I was in your discussion of *Twelfth Night*. It was so intelligent.
TERRY: Oh, thank you very much. I'm afraid that the rest of the inmates didn't share your enthusiasm.
CATHERINE: Barbarians! They've had no training, my dear, no training. Why, when I played in *Twelfth Night*—

TERRY: Oh, did you play in *Twelfth Night?*
CATHERINE: Yes, I—I have a few of my notices here if you'd care
to see them . . . Oh how lucky, they're right on top.

In *her* middle age Collier gained a reputation for being the best
acting coach in Hollywood and helped a number of actors make the
transition from silent films to talkies. By the time she and Hepburn
became acquainted, she was elderly. Luckily for Hepburn, she still
lived in an era when old people were thought to be wise. Hepburn
respected Collier for her immense experience, her long and vast
knowledge. Now, of course, anyone in any field who has too much
experience is dismissed as being old school, or by virtue of his or her
hard-earned wisdom, incapable of thinking outside the box.

This brings us to a matter I can't, in good conscience, over-
look. Hepburn may have been as fearful as the rest of us, but obvi-
ously she is not the rest of us. I feel safe in saying there is no
middle-aged movie star reading this who is faced with the task of
re-creating herself as a great Shakespearean actress. Nicole Kid-
man, if you *are* reading this, my apologies. I'm sure you will do fine.

Most of us have more mundane fears than those of Katharine
Hepburn. They are no less fear-inducing for their lack of world-
class glamour. We are average men and women contemplating the
prospect of going back to school to finish our degrees or earn a
new one; starting up that computer business with our modest in-
heritance that our wife secretly, or not so secretly, believes could be
put to better use; accepting that promotion at work, even though it

means traveling to Cincinnati twice a month; leaving our lout of a husband; joining the Peace Corps; coming out to our father; standing up to our mother; renting the basement out to our pot-smoking brother who means well.

HOW HEPBURN FOUND THE COURAGE

1. Hepburn was an early practitioner of deodorant-television-commercial wisdom: **never let anyone see you sweat**. "The first thing to learn is that nobody must ever know how terrified you are. You've got to be absolutely cool . . . although you may be dying." Paradoxically, if you never let anyone else see you sweat, you don't notice it much yourself, which makes you feel less afraid.

2. **Act as if.** William James, philosopher and older brother of Henry James, was fond of the saying "If you want a quality, act as if you already had it." Hepburn acted as if she were an actress for many years before she actually became one. You could even argue she won her first Oscar while she was still acting as if.

3. **"Stride on!"** One of the great Hepburn coping mechanisms was pushing forward without giving a thought to what she was doing. The *Dick Cavett Show* interview is the perfect example. She plopped down in that chair, threw her foot up on the table, and said, "Go now."

4. Disrespect your fear. Imagine your fear has no clothes on. Pretend your fear is the dog's favorite chew toy. Call your fear bad names; imagine it bursting into racking sobs. Refuse to acknowledge that which is making you tremble. If necessary, **pretend you're in Indianapolis**.

5. **Get used to it.** I truly wish #5 wasn't the way it usually goes. Into her fifties Hepburn continued on with Shakespeare and also tackled both Eugene O'Neill and Shaw. Fear didn't prevent her from earning a reputation as America's greatest classical actress.

Her arch-nemesis, Brooks Atkinson, didn't have much good to say about Hepburn's *As You Like It*, but also points out, "Most commercial Shakespearean productions are put on as if the producers were very much afraid that the audiences would not like Shakespeare." One reviewer had the nerve to quip that Hepburn's comely gams were as good as her iambs.

Hepburn went on to play in *The Merchant of Venice*, *Measure for Measure*, *The Taming of the Shrew*, *Much Ado About Nothing*, and *Twelfth Night*. In 1957, at age fifty, she played the famous young seductress Cleopatra in *Antony and Cleopatra* at the Stratford, Connecticut, Shakespeare Theatre, to great acclaim. Hepburn may have feared forgetting her lines or losing control of her voice or seeming inauthentic, but what continues to amaze is that she was not afraid of that most terrifying thing: aging in the public eye.

9

THINKING LIKE A LEGEND

*"Who Is Katharine Hepburn? It Took Me a Long Time to Create
That Creature."*

Since *Time* recently named You, meaning Us, its 2006 Person of
the Year, it's important that we figure out how to become legendary, fast, or get lost in the shuffle of the millions of other hon-
orees who are using the World Wide Web to make their claim to
fame. Just because we People of the Year now possess a free forum
and a global audience, that doesn't mean we're intriguing, or that
what we have to say will be remembered.

To be legendary is to be admired, talked about (in a good
way), emulated, and respected. The test of one's legendary status
is the degree to which one is forgiven bad behavior and egregious
mistakes.

Which brings us immediately to the fantastic spectacle of
Coco, a musical based on the life of the chic French fashion designer Coco Chanel, with music by André Previn, book and lyrics
by Alan Jay Lerner, and starring Katharine Hepburn, a star of the

stage and screen who couldn't sing, couldn't really dance, despite her great athleticism, and cared nothing for fashion. It was an audacious act of miscasting. Hepburn talked her way through the songs, not unlike how Rex Harrison was forced to do in *My Fair Lady*. In Chanel's trademark big, round black-framed glasses and black cloche hat, Hepburn managed to look like the Marx Brothers' long-lost sister.

And yet, the Mark Hellinger Theater, where the play opened in late 1969, enjoyed the largest box-office advance in Broadway history. The reviews lauded Hepburn for her élan, her vitality, her chutzpah. Audiences loved her, rewarding her for just being Hepburn.

Clive Barnes, in the *New York Times*, called her singing voice "a neat mixture of faith, love and laryngitis, unforgettable, unbelievable and delightful." Walter Kerr called the play "a showcase, a form of endearment, a gesture of assent, an open palm of respect."

Hepburn had been far better in other plays and many other films, but for the first time in her life she felt the audience was on her side and that she could do no wrong. She was right, of course. By the age of sixty-two she'd become a legend.

There were other great actresses and actors of Hepburn's vintage who never became legends. Tracy was legendary among actors and admired by the public, but he never made the leap to cultural icon. Perhaps he was too plain. Joan Crawford and Bette Davis were legendary actresses, but they were not legendary heroines. Talk show hosts never claimed they possessed secrets to the art of living. Perhaps they neglected to be peculiar enough (or were peculiar in the wrong way). Maybe too much was known about their personal lives. Then there was the business of succumbing in late-middle age to starring in cheesy horror movies. The same year Hepburn was playing Mary Tyrone in Eugene O'Neill's masterpiece *Long Day's Journey into Night*, Joan and Bette costarred in the sensationally campy *What Ever Happened to Baby Jane?* The movie was a hit—really, you can't look away—but the price Crawford and Davis paid was steep. Overnight they became too old and freakish (but not in a good way) to be relevant. They were terrific, but they wound up seeming pathetic, and thus not worthy of mythologizing.

Hepburn always had one eye on her career and another on how it was being perceived. She knew intuitively the tremendous importance of creating, and tapping into, a self that was larger-than-life, a self that would shield her more vulnerable self, while at the same time be perfect for public consumption.

During the making of *The African Queen*, a film that defined the middle-aged Kate in the same way *The Philadelphia Story* had codified the young Kate, Bogie watched her rush around the jungle in the equatorial heat with dizzying Hepburnian high energy, locating a golf course, making appointments with the local tree purveyor to see a tree felled, or going with John Huston to hunt boar, and said, "Here is either a twenty-four-karat nut, or a great actress working mighty hard at being one."

Bogie—also a legend—knew the antics of another legend when he saw them.

◆—◆—◆

Working hard was what Hepburn did, had always done, would always do. At the end of her life it would defeat her, this obsession with striding ever on, but her staunch work ethic was one of the reasons we loved her. Hepburn was, for several generations, the embodiment of one facet of the American dream. She wanted to be a famous actress, and even though she was not conventionally pretty or even a particularly good actor, through dint of hard work, perseverance, believing in herself, and a refusal to compromise her principles, Hepburn became one of the world's great stars.

Her more recent biographers have maintained that Kate was never as naïve and well-intentioned as we assumed, that she was also shrewd and calculating. Sure, she owned the traits we all admired, but she was also intent on making sure we appreciated them. She was determined always to appear unstudied and unselfconscious.

Someone born after 1985 will have to take it from here . . . I've lost track of who comes after Generation Y, but people in their twenties would surely understand Hepburn's hyperawareness of her own image. From the moment of their videotaped birth through every dutifully taped and annotated "first" (crawl up the stairs, stagger across the room on chubby toddler legs, recitation of ABCs, holiday pageant, soccer game) to this very second, where somewhere someone is agonizing over the impression his viewer base will glean from the songs he chooses to list as favorites on his Facebook page, concerns about self-presentation are a way of life.

To young adults, it makes absolute sense that an actress of Hepburn's caliber would manipulate the press to her advantage, or would avoid having her picture taken with the intention of spurring photographers into working even harder to grab a shot of her, or would selectively edit her past to create one impression rather than another. They wouldn't understand that their elders had a lot invested in thinking that the Hepburn they saw on the screen, and playing Coco Chanel, and even beating a rug on the sidewalk outside her Turtle Bay town house, was the same Kate that existed in real life.

—•—

USEFUL TIPS FOR CREATING YOUR OWN CREATURE

Information Management

For most of her life Hepburn enjoyed an undeserved reputation for despising the press. Until the early seventies, when she decided her stubborn decades-long practice of privacy was in itself a tool to be used, she spurned interviews or, when she was forced to endure them, told out-and-out lies. Or, she was a plain old pain in the ass. When asked a harmless question, she would say, "Now that's a damn silly question. Unless you've got something more intelligent than that to say, we can end this right now."

Hepburn was a competitor, a trickster. She loved nothing more than a good tall tale, tossed at a reporter like a water balloon over the backyard fence during the neighbors' party, just to see what would happen. Just because Hepburn wouldn't help the press by making its job easier, that didn't mean she didn't respect it, or what it could do for her. She was as natural at playing the press as any hard-nosed studio press agent.

Over her career she was often awarded the Hollywood Women's Press Club Sour Apple Award, an annual "prize" bestowed on Hollywood's least cooperative actor. Hepburn won so many times she is said to have lost count (although that seems unlikely). Rochelle Hudson won the award for Most Cooperative Actor the greatest number of times. Ms. Hudson appeared in 119 films. Her most famous role was that of Natalie Wood's mother in *Rebel Without a Cause*. Her last movie was *Dr. Terror's Gallery of Horrors*. You can see where being cooperative got her.

In the later part of the last century, when Hepburn decided to come clean on a number of topics, including her short marriage to long-suffering Luddy, she described herself as being "an absolute pig" to him, knowing her harsh self-assessment would absolve her. In talking about her disdain for the Oscars, and her refusal to attend the ceremony and receive her award, she castigated herself for behaving boorishly. Hepburn was an expert at being candid when it would have little real effect on her or anyone else.

The Art of Misdirection
In her early years Hepburn thought nothing of straight-out lying to the press. The rest of her life she employed a more sophisticated form of misdirection. Mostly, she allowed people to think what they wanted, as opposed to actively spreading untruths.

When forced to comply, she deflected questions about her

age, about her plans, about Tracy. In this way, she allowed misconceptions to grow around her like pernicious weeds. Perhaps she learned to do this at the feet of her dashing agent/love interest Leland Hayward. In 1934 when the ill-conceived *The Little Minister* followed on the heels of the just plain strange *Spitfire*, Hepburn still enjoyed a lot of glowing press because Hayward made sure everyone knew he and Hepburn were on the verge of getting married. Then and now, nothing helps a star's career more than a romance played out in public.

Allowing the world to be misled creates something else that's in increasingly short supply of late: mystery. You cannot be a legend, even among your college drinking buddies, without maintaining at least a minor sense of mystery. "Where were you last night?" is only an interesting question when it remains unanswered.

It's maddening, really, that for everything that's been written about Hepburn, questions basic to our knowledge of her remain unanswered. Did she really think her parents were perfect? (we suspect she must have resented her father); was Laura Harding the true love of her life? (possibly, depending on whom you talk to); and what about her "thing" with Spencer Tracy? So ill-defined was that relationship, we still can't quite decide what to call it.

When Hepburn was in Australia touring with the Old Vic, she met a woman who became her friend, and to whom she confessed that her birthday was not November 8, as she'd told everyone for all those years, but May 12. November 8 was the birthday of her dead brother, Tom. Hepburn told the woman that she'd lied because she needed to have secrets.

There's Nothing Wrong with Being a Little Disingenuous

We forget that Hepburn was the daughter of a politician. Kit Hepburn was an expert at appearing feminine and nonthreatening while pressing her feminist causes. Hepburn remarked that one aspect of her mother's genius was to invite her enemies to tea, wherein she would dress beautifully and make her case while serving the sandwiches.

Hepburn's political expertise can be seen in *All About Me*, the 1993 made-for-TV-documentary, in which a brusque and confident eighty-six-year-old Hepburn takes us on a quick swing through her long life. She has her talking points down. She mentions everything she's been accused of—selfishness, dedication to being a famous movie star, "living like a man." When in need of an adjective, Hepburn always preferred a superlative. People are stupid or absolutely fascinating; they're idiots or completely wonderful.

She claims her career was due to sheer luck, that it was her good fortune to have been born during a time when her attributes were in vogue. This is pure Hepburn dissembling. Twenty-five years earlier, after she won back-to-back Best Actress Oscars and realized she was being deified, she said in an interview with a London paper, "Now that I am Saint Katharine, it is fashionable to say that I am a beauty with a well-proportioned face. But when I was beginning, they thought I was a freak with all those freckles."

By 1993, however, she was gracious to pretend her life's achievements were the result of luck, and terribly sweet, terribly wonderful people helping her along the way. All beguiling nonsense. Still, we loved it.

Know When to Shut Up

I cannot put too fine a point on it. To become a legend, whether it be to millions of adoring fans or your nearest and dearest, one must know when to shut up. To this day, part of Hepburn's sturdy, enduring appeal is that she admitted little, white-lied a lot, and allowed people to think what they wanted.

Rewrite Your Own History

Hepburn cherished her personal history. I'm hard-pressed to think of another legendary star whose childhood totems are more universally well-known: the feisty Yankees Kit and Hep; the happy summers at Fenwick; the sports competitions; the troubles and eventual triumphs at Bryn Mawr. The older Hepburn got, the higher and shinier the gloss on her past became. And so what.

The most burnished chapter in her life was that of her relationship with Tracy, which underwent heavy editing and revising. Friends were shocked when the obsessively private and principled Hepburn agreed to collaborate on *The Spencer Tracy Legacy: A Tribute by Katharine Hepburn*. It was an all-star tribute to the old man, with fond reminiscences from Sidney Poitier, Frank Sinatra, Lee Marvin, Elizabeth Taylor, and many others. Hepburn's narration is pure treacle. She swooned and cooed and dove into her bag of superlatives in a way that made everyone squirm. She was determined, apparently, to make sure her love affair with Spencer was going to be viewed as one of the great love stories in the history of the known world. Now that Louise Tracy had died, Hepburn didn't see any reason why she couldn't tell her highly embellished side of things, helping along the process whereby legend is turned into fact.

The great sidekick of her middle age, Irene Selznick, took issue with what she viewed as Hepburn's bad taste, and their friendship was never the same. Still, to this day, when people remember Hepburn, they always remember her abiding, unusual love for Tracy.

•—◆—•

Bette Davis said, in what might well be the greatest understatement in the English language, that aging is not for sissies. It's one of the great raw deals of human existence; we are old for so much longer than we are young, and old is a place no one wants to be. As the sage Nora Ephron so succinctly put it, aging sucks. To our American way of thinking, to say there's no way around it seems defeatist. To voluntarily hang up our spurs is tantamount to cutting and running on our own lives. It's decadent and European to admit you're too old to keep up. But to keep on living with vigor in our seventies, eighties, and upward requires a degree of fortitude, courage, realism, and humor that's beyond most of us, including Katharine Hepburn.

There's no question that the less than young among us should fall down on our knees in gratitude for the way in which Hepburn broadened the horizons of midlife. She made it not just permissible to be older than twenty-eight, she succeeded in making it look stylish. She won her second Oscar at age sixty, her third at sixty-one, and her fourth at seventy-four. I'm safe in saying that she was the first American woman who lived the life of someone a full decade younger, and thus contributed to the establishment of the great contemporary cliché: sixty is the new fifty, fifty is the new forty, et cetera.

That said, it is my duty to report that old age did not suit Hepburn. The last years of her life were uncommonly sad and poignant. In an effort to ward off decrepitude, she made a handful of third-rate television movies that don't even deserve mention. Even more unfortunate, she set about securing her legend for posterity without admitting—or perhaps understanding—that was what she was up to.

Hepburn had first tinkered with her much vaunted privacy on the Cavett show. The alleged reason behind her appearance was to promote her new film, *A Delicate Balance*. It seems she consented because it finally dawned on her that television was here to stay. It was the world's first extended exposure to the unscripted Kate the Great and even now is worth watching for Cavett's unabashed delight at having captured the unicorn.

Kate gives a magnificent performance of Hepburn. She is down-to-earth, playful, funny, smart, opinionated, both girlish and dignified. The then newly released Hepburn quips and anecdotes that would become codified and increasingly hoary over the years shone bright with cagey wisdom. She was still circumspect about her relationship with Spencer, although she did praise his acting with shining eyes.

Cavett admits to her at the end of the interview that he fell in

love with her at least seven times during their two evenings together. It was both historic and lovely.

A new world opened up for Hepburn; she would talk to the
press. She would be absolutely adorable, charming, fascinating,
giving interviews hither and thither, allowing every reporter to be
gracious to her for violating her privacy, which was now a thing of
the past. She would trot out the same stories. She would crank out
a few books herself—*The Making of "The African Queen"* in 1987 and
four years later the dashed-off *Me: Stories of My Life*.

In 1983 she invited biographer A. Scott Berg into her life for
reasons that for all her legendary directness, she never made clear.
Berg had written well-received biographies of book editor Maxwell
Perkins, movie mogul Samuel Goldwyn, and Charles Lindbergh,
and contacted Hepburn about interviewing her for *Esquire*. He
never pretended to be anything but a lifelong fan. The story never
ran in the magazine, but a twenty-year "friendship" eventuated. In
exchange for being admitted to the inner circle, Berg would be the
one-man audience for the Katharine Hepburn show (she joked
with him that an interview is actually a performance). He would
watch her swim in Long Island Sound in twelve-degree weather,
make her Scotch and sodas to her exact specifications, suffer the
brunt of her bad temper and cruel remarks, and marvel at hearing
the same stories she'd told Dick Cavett.

Still, in all the years of their great friendship, the great outspoken Hepburn never once said, "Look here, Mr. Berg, I'm not
going to be around forever, and I'm going to need a proper biographer and you're my man." She didn't because she couldn't face that

she'd reached a place in her life where it made sense to begin looking back. (Berg's memoir of having known Hepburn, *Kate Remembered*, was rushed into print several weeks after her death. No one
knew quite what to make of it.)

Me: Stories of My Life, Hepburn's own long-awaited autobiography—with the exception of the final, moving page-and-
a-half-long chapter, in which she addresses Tracy—is one long,
dashed-out recapitulation of legend without an ounce of reflec-
tion or introspection. For her entire life Hepburn subscribed to
the theory that any thought deeper than a rain puddle was "making a fuss" and here is the proof.

Me is Hepburn doing her Hepburn impersonation. Given her
pride in her Bryn Mawr education, and her professed respect for
proper English, one would think she would have taken time to
compose a more formal autobiography. Of her deep friendship
with the inestimable director John Ford, one would think she
could rouse herself to say more about his passing than "tough—
loved his friends—hated his enemies—loved Ireland—loved the
film business—loved his hits—adored his failures—perverse-
stubborn—relentless—arrogant—and a great friend."

Could you imagine if Hepburn attacked the task of writing
a proper autobiography in the same manner she'd plunged into
mastering Shakespeare thirty years earlier? She could have spent a
year reading the world's great autobiographies. She could have
repaired to Fenwick with her buckets of flowers, lit a fire, and
cracked open *The Education of Henry Adams* or Booker T. Washing-
ton's *Up from Slavery*. She would never have touched a book with

the title *Confessions of an English Opium Eater* (by the great fruit-cake Thomas De Quincey), but how about Winston Churchill's *My Early Life: 1874–1904?*

Impossible.

◆—◆

In the final phase of her film career, it was no longer necessary for Hepburn to focus only on roles that were written for her. Both *Rooster Cogburn* (1975) and *On Golden Pond* (1981) were scripts that called for Hepburn to play Katharine Hepburn playing determined old ladies with high morals and fierce opinions. In *Rooster Cogburn*, which should rightly have been called *The African Queen II*, Hepburn is Eula Goodnight, a missionary's daughter who hooks up with John Wayne's Rooster Cogburn (whom we met in the far better *True Grit*). After Eula's ancient father is murdered by bad guys at their far-flung outpost, Rooster shows up and off they go together, trading barbs, having moments, and riding a raft loaded with nitroglycerin down some puny rapids. Hepburn, who was sixty-eight, did her own horseback riding, and since *Rooster Cogburn* was a John Wayne western, you can bet there was a lot of it. The dialogue brings to mind Fran Lebowitz's observation that the opposite of talking isn't listening, it's waiting. Hepburn waits for Wayne to stop grumbling tough-guy platitudes out of the side of his mouth so that she can drop a few sharp Hepburn bons mots; then Wayne waits for Hepburn to stop dropping her sharp bons mots so he can grumble another tough-guy platitude out of the side of his mouth.

The world adored *On Golden Pond*. Hepburn and Fonda—for the record, they are Ethel and Norman Thayer—play a couple on the threshold of eighty, married for fifty years. Jane Fonda, duly aerobicized, plays their only daughter, Chelsea. On the first day of filming, Hepburn gave Fonda Spencer Tracy's old brown fedora, which he wore for the rest of the movie and probably aided Hepburn in delivering a pitch-perfect performance as crotchety Norman's resilient and adoring wife. Can anyone forget her quavery voice telling Henry he's her knight in shining armor? Both Fonda and Hepburn won Oscars; Fonda's first and only, Hepburn's record-breaking fourth.

It was Fonda's last movie, and many people who hung in there with Hepburn through all of her subsequent made-for-TV movies wished it had also been Kate's last. The TV movies weren't lousy, they were just beneath her. Watching them, you want to shout at the screen, "Please! Stop! Stop in the name of who you were. Let us remember the hilarious you in *Bringing Up Baby*; the gorgeous, sassy, cool-yet-hot you of *The Philadelphia Story* and *Woman of the Year*; the stalwart, endearing you of *The African Queen*! Then, you watch some more and you think, "Damn, girl, you are *never* going to give up, are you? Right on."

Hepburn claimed she had no fear of death. She didn't believe in an afterlife and thought dying would just be a good long sleep. It's all bull, of course. If she were so sanguine, why did she continue making forgettable movies that would contribute nothing to the landmark oeuvre she'd spent her entire life creating? The fear of having nothing to do, of course. The day you stop pushing your-self ever forward, you might be forced to sit still and think.

It's one of the pitfalls of believing work is the cure for every-thing that ails you. Hepburn's way of facing her inevitable decline was doing the same thing she'd done since the day she arrived in Hollywood in 1932: she made one wretched movie after the next.

Quality was no longer the point. In middle age, during her classical period, she'd been concerned with quality; by the time she was old she just wanted to keep the machine going. She once said, "As for me, prizes are nothing. My prize is my work." At the end, we had no choice but to believe her.

Still, it's hard to forgive Hepburn's creaky cameo in Warren Beatty's 1994 *Love Affair*. She played Beatty's eccentric aunt, who lived on a hillside in Tahiti, or somewhere. She delivered an incom-prehensible speech about ducks. She was eighty-seven. She was tiny and frail and broke our hearts by reminding us that human be-ings can be very old for a very long time.

After that, we saw little of her. She left her New York town house and moved to Fenwick. Years before she'd been forced to give up golf and tennis, and she'd become inactive and plump. She'd grown to enjoy her Scotch rather much. Because she'd lived a life of rude good health and frantic activity, in her old age she was at a loss. She was not a philanthropist, nor was she Constance Col-lier, who at the end of her life became a mentor and teacher to younger actors. If Hepburn taught, it was by example only. She'd placed all her eggs in the basket of her magnificent physical self that presumed her ability to swim in Long Island Sound in January whenever the spirit moved her. Dylan Thomas would have approved: Hepburn was not about to go gentle, but raged against the dying light. Katharine Hepburn died at 2:50 P.M. on June 29, 2003. Her ashes are buried in Hartford's Cedar Hill Cemetery. At her request, they were placed not beside those of her parents, but beside her brother Tom's.

10

TWENTY-TWO WAYS TO GET YOUR HEPBURN ON

Our Modern Fear of Striding On; The Price of So Many Options;
Suggestions for Getting On with It by Getting Our Hepburn On; Have a Credo,
Waste Time, et Cetera

—◦•◦—

Not long ago I was in line at a movie theater eavesdropping on a conversation between a woman and her male friend. I had the impression that they'd known each other for a long time, because she was ranting in the manner women usually reserve for their girlfriends. They were both in their mid-thirties, I guessed. She was the sort of fresh-faced young woman you see around occasionally these days; you could tell she was smart, competent, and detail-oriented. She wasn't the dreamy sort. She looked to be the type who wasn't late on her bills and tried to keep up on current events. She looked decent, in her low-rise jeans, scuffed black boots, cable-knit sweater. Her friend was dressed almost identically. He carried a messenger bag. This is all I remember about him because he almost never spoke.

She, on the other hand, was frantic. She was a thinker, an ago-
nizer, a person who spent the wee hours weighing her pros and
cons, of which there were an endless number. She was in a state, agonizing over whether she should marry the guy she was seeing, go
back to school for her master's degree, take a friend up on her offer
to do something or other in Barcelona—I think it was Barcelona,
maybe it was Basel—or take the marketing job at that software
company in San Diego. She had never been to San Diego. And
what about all the stress this was causing? She knew she needed to
get back to yoga, but how could she when she needed to figure out
what to do with her life?

Her friend said he didn't know, that she just needed to decide
and go for it.

That's when she cried out in anguish that it wasn't a matter of
deciding, it was a matter of knowing what she *should* be doing, and
the thing that was driving her mad was that she felt as if she should
be doing all of it.

He tried again. He said she should count herself lucky to have
so many options. I could tell she didn't appreciate his reasonable-
ness. "They don't feel like options! I feel like no matter what I do,
it's the wrong thing," she said, sounding as if she was on the verge
of tears. So upset was she, even the ticket seller, half asleep behind
her Plexiglas shield, perked right up. As the young woman slid her
twenty through the slot in the ticket window, I noticed her nails,
bitten to the quick.

It would make for a nice thematic transition to report we

were standing in line for a Katharine Hepburn double feature, one where this young woman could see Hepburn conquer the world without breaking a sweat. But double features have gone the way of dial phones, and aside from the occasional revival theater, the only place you can see *Bringing Up Baby* or *The Philadelphia Story* is to rent it on DVD.

Instead, we were seeing a movie adapted from a comic book, where the characters all look like personal trainers with supernatural powers (have you ever noticed there are no out-of-shape superheroes?). I imagined this movie would not provide escape for the woman suffering from having so many options, but only serve to remind her that these days the only women who seem to live their lives with aplomb are those born with the ability to see through walls or levitate.

It's the signature malady of our age: feeling, at any given time, as if you should be doing something else, and as if by not doing that something else you've either made the wrong decision or somehow violated our modern rules for living a full and meaningful life. We question everything, we doubt our decisions, we are never beautiful enough. Our lives lack meaning. Our bank accounts lack the necessary amount of figures. If we are happy, we wonder if it's genuine happiness, or perhaps we're just *settling*. We long for meaning, but don't recognize meaning when it falls on our head.

I should have turned right around and told that young woman she needed to get her Hepburn on.

Indeed, were I more like Katharine Hepburn, I would have.

TIPS FOR GETTING YOUR HEPBURN ON

1. Have a Credo

Hepburn found her credo in the house in Hartford where she lived as a child. The previous owner had had the words LISTEN TO THE SONG OF LIFE cut into the stone mantel. It sounds Walt Whitman-esque, like something he might have done when he was bored of listening to the Song of Himself. It's got everything a credo should have: it's poetic, empowering, upbeat, and a bit opaque. The author of Hepburn's credo was one Mabel Collins (1851–1927), a theosophist, medium, and author of *Light on the Path*, in which the saying first appeared. Miss Collins was also a fashion writer and claimed to be the lover of Jack the Ripper. Adopting a credo is key, because it indicates you believe your life is grand enough to warrant one. "Everything I do is the wrong thing" is not a good credo.

2. Find Yourself Fascinating

Hepburn said, "Stone-cold sober, I find myself absolutely fascinating." As most of us are very far from feeling this way, it's safe to lift the ban on being sober, I should think. You may think yourself fascinating after a glass of pinot. The important thing is that you view your qualities and quirks, your challenges and achievements, with real interest. Appreciate yourself. This sounds easier than it is. Most of us secretly feel about ourselves as did Groucho, that we would never want to belong to a club that would have us as a member.

3. Find a Sport(s)

Hepburn was the living example of the benefits of regular exercise. Long before there were special hundred-dollar shoes to run in and special exercise classes in which you could pretend you were a stripper, there was Hepburn, swimming, golfing, and playing tennis (she was what we now call a cross-trainer). She was rarely sick, never fat, didn't seem to suffer any chronic ailments, and always looked younger than her years (except for the skin thing, see below). Spencer Tracy, in comparison, never got any exercise except what Hepburn forced on him, suffered from emphysema, heart disease, and other problems related to his preferred activity: sitting around drinking Irish whiskey. He died of heart failure at sixty-seven. Should you remain unconvinced about the benefits of regular, lifelong exercise, consider this: Both Tracy and Hepburn were big smokers. Hepburn smoked two packs a day* for over twenty years, and she still almost lived to be a hundred.

4. Say What You Think

Most of us worry too much about how what we have to say is going to be received. Then, we tailor our thoughts to meet the expectations of the person to whom we're speaking. If you're a

---

*Hepburn quit smoking on the first try. Her technique: First give up the cigarette of the day you enjoy the least, say, the one before breakfast. Do that for a week. Then give up the next one you enjoy least, say, the one after a cup of tea in the afternoon. Do that for a week. Keep giving up the one you enjoy least, until there are none.

doctor delivering a bad diagnosis to someone, this is a good skill to embrace (although I'm sure Hepburn would argue you should just spit it out and not beat around the bush). Too much thought-tailoring over time eventually leads to not knowing what we really think, which is the first step to losing track of who we really are.

5. Don't Confuse Self-Improvement with Self-Remodeling

Hepburn was always trying to improve herself. A self-confessed compulsive worker, she made herself into a great actress from a curious-looking girl who had a flair for self-dramatization and that was about it. But she never tried to *change* herself. We live in a time when television, magazines, newspapers, the Internet—every medium you can name—streams the same message: that to be happy you must work to change yourself. Women have gone from eternally remodeling the living room to eternally remodeling themselves. Right now: do a self-assessment of everything good, bad, or indifferent you've got going for you and see #2.

6. Realize You Can Go Forward Blindly

You don't always have to know what you're getting into in order to succeed. Hepburn admitted that she was a tremendous "flash reader." She could memorize a part after reading it through once, then laugh and cry on cue without having a clue what she was doing. This seemed to have little bearing on whether she gave a good performance or a bad one.

7. Assume the Answer Is No, Unless You Can Find a Reason to Say Yes

In our time we feel that unless we say yes to everything from helping our brother move to skydiving lessons to marrying someone we don't know well that we're either not being a good person, or we're missing out on something. The result is usually resentment and regrets. Hepburn, on the other hand, made it a policy to say no. No, I won't star in *Mother Carey's Chickens*. No, I don't want to talk to the reporter. No, I don't want to marry you, sign your picture, allow that stunt double to dive into the frigid lake when I am perfectly able to do it myself. As a result, Hepburn experienced a life of few regrets and no real resentment that we can tell. She said yes only when she couldn't think of a good reason to keep saying no.

8. Be Frugal

Most of us do not have fathers who are willing to manage our money and give us an allowance until we are fifty-five, thus ensuring we don't make a mess of our finances. Still, when we remember that Hepburn was never forced to do anything she didn't want to for lack of funds, it's worth trying to cultivate our own inner penny-pinching dad. Kate's frugality, as imposed by Hep, allowed her to do Shakespeare for $350 a week and say no to doing dairy-creamer commercials in her dotage. (Unlike poor Steve Allen.)

9. Strive to Fully Inhabit Your Life

Long before Harvard professor Richard Alpert dropped acid, became Ram Dass, and started a movement, Hepburn, who had nothing good to say about hippies, advocated the philosophy of be here now.

10. Prefer Dark Chocolate

Hepburn enjoyed her chocolate, especially almond bark. She also routinely ate five vegetables at dinner. Perhaps, like me, you find this interesting because you never realized there were five vegetables.

11. Develop a Concept of Fun That Includes Not Just Play, but Work

If you love your job, you'll never work a day in your life, or so said Confucius. Hepburn loved to work. She loved to *clean* (I have nothing edifying to say about that). She found every aspect of moviemaking to be a lark, from reworking the script to figuring out whether the snaps on her sleeves were going to trip her up during the scene where she throws off her coat. Expanding your notion of fun beyond a two-week vacation in Maui increases the chances you'll have more of it.

12. Find Danger Exhilarating

In *The African Queen* after the drunken Charlie and the prim Rose survive the rapids, Rosie is flushed and breathless. She blots her cheeks with her hands and breathes, "I never dreamed that any mere physical experience could be so stimulating." It was old news to Hepburn, who was taught to ride her bike by Hep, who took her to the top of a hill, plopped her on the seat, and let go.

13. Master the Headstand, and Keep the Skill Sharp as Long as Possible
At age eighty-four Hepburn claimed she could still stand on her head, walk on her hands, and perform a one-and-a-half off the diving board.

14. Wear Sunscreen
Hepburn was a genuine redhead, with a redhead's freckled complexion. She spent her life baking in the sun and paid a steep price. The first sunscreen was invented in 1936 by chemist Eugene Schueller, who founded L'Oréal. Hepburn traveled in Hollywood circles. Certainly a makeup woman or Laura Harding or *someone* must have gotten a look at her fragile skin that was always ruddy with sunburn and told her to slather some on, for God sakes. By her forties, her skin was shot. Not just freckly, but blotchy, peeling, and piebald. It was a mess. She had repeated surgeries to remove this mole and that weird patch, to no avail. It made her look not simply old, but alien.

15. I Cannot Emphasize This Enough, WEAR SUNSCREEN
She suffered from melanoma, too.

16. Find the Type of Clothes You Feel Best In and Never Take Them Off
Hepburn revolutionized the way we dress. You are probably wearing what you are wearing right now because Hepburn refused to be a good girl and put on a dress. The thing is, for you, wearing a dress might be what you're all about. A miniskirt and tights might say "you" more than slacks and a button-down shirt. If that's the case,

reject the slacks. Buy every miniskirt you can get your hands on (well, maybe not every; see #8). There's a popular fashion makeover show that purports to help women look sharp while developing their own style, but every last makeover candidate always winds up in pointy shoes and a snappy jacket. Not that there's anything wrong with pointy shoes and a snappy jacket, but perhaps you would never be caught dead in pointy shoes. If so, make it a mission to avoid them your entire life. The same holds true for makeup. Hepburn never wore a stitch, with the exception of that devastating red lipstick.

17. Cold Baths, Pros and Cons

I never quite got Hepburn's obsession with cold water. I suspect it's just a version of the joke generations of fourth-graders always find so funny about the guy who hit himself in the head with a hammer because it felt so good when he stopped.

Ocean swimming in Long Island Sound aside, she also preferred hypothermia-inducing baths and showers. The cold shower has long been considered a folk remedy in India (where it is sweltering year-round). The alleged benefits of the blue-lip bath include increased circulation throughout the body, reduction of blood pressure, strengthening of the mucous membranes (helps prevent colds), and cleansing of the circulatory system. How a cold shower accomplishes the latter is anyone's guess.

18. Surprise the World and Yourself by Enjoying a Good Cry

Hepburn was both tough and emotional. At Humphrey Bogart's funeral she wore a dress, and when she glimpsed a model of *The*

Santana, his cherished sailboat, on the altar, she burst into tears and wept like a three-year-old.

19. Waste Time

Alas, the icon Hepburn did not have all the answers to life. While industry and an astounding work ethic offers the perfect antidote to the sloth and slackitude that seem to have infected the citizens of the world's developed nations, the woman could really have used some downtime. And I don't mean an evening of playing the smack-down Parcheesi games she and her siblings seemed to have enjoyed at Fenwick, where accusations flew and the game usually ended when someone stomped off in a rage. At the end of her life she was quite cantankerous, and I can't help feeling that if she'd taken a yearly cruise, her disposition would have been much sunnier. She will probably come back from the grave and call me an idiot, but work is *not* the cure-all for everything. Sometimes, you just need to stare out the window.

20. Never Pass Up the Opportunity to Give Someone a Good Sock in the Jaw

On the set of *The Lion in Winter*, Peter O'Toole was hogging the makeup man when Hepburn needed him. O'Toole didn't have a scene that day, and Hepburn did. She sent for the makeup man, who failed to appear. She marched down to O'Toole's dressing room, threw open the door, and gave him a good slug. She told him, "'The next time I send for the makeup man, send him!' So I went back, roaring with laughter. I really socked him. He was dumbfounded. Did him a lot of good, I think. It does everyone good to be hit."

21. *Care for Someone Who Doesn't Deserve It*

No one will ever know the truth about what went on between Tracy and Hepburn. She, who refused to live five minutes in the past, who believed that when something was done it was done, continued to rent Tracy's guesthouse on George Cukor's estate for eleven years after Tracy's death. Unlike Hep, who couldn't get rid of Kit's things fast enough, Hepburn kept everything in Tracy's cottage exactly as it was. Perhaps Hepburn's devotion was like the Tin Man's journey with Dorothy to Oz; in the process she earned herself a heart.

22. *Make It Count*

ACKNOWLEDGMENTS

Words fail me when it comes to expressing my gratitude to Kim Witherspoon and David Forrer of Inkwell Management; Karen Rinaldi, Lindsay Sagnette, Greg Villepique, Yelena Gitlin, Alona Fryman, and the ever-patient Melanie Cecka, all of Bloomsbury; Steve Boldt, copy editor par excellence; Danna Schaeffer, friend, wit, and perfect reader; and Dr. Rick Jewel at the USC School of Cinema, in whose class I first saw *Bringing Up Baby*.

This book would not exist without the support, love, good jokes, and meal-cooking of Jerrod Allen. And finally, where would I be without my girl, Fiona?

A READING LIST

KATHARINE HEPBURN

Andersen, Christopher. *An Affair to Remember: The Remarkable Love Story of Katharine Hepburn and Spencer Tracy.* New York: William Morrow, 1997.

Andersen, Christopher. *Young Kate.* New York: Henry Holt, 1988.

Berg, A. Scott. *Kate Remembered.* New York: G. P. Putnam's Sons, 2003.

Britton, Andrew. *Katharine Hepburn: Star as Feminist.* New York: Columbia University Press, 2003.

Edwards, Anne. *A Remarkable Woman: A Biography of Katharine Hepburn.* New York: William Morrow, 1985.

Hepburn, Katharine. *Me: Stories of My Life.* New York: Alfred A. Knopf, 1991.

Hepburn, Katharine. *The Making of "The African Queen," or, How I Went to Africa with Bogart, Bacall and Huston and Almost Lost My Mind.* New York: Alfred A. Knopf, 1987.

Higham, Charles. *Kate: The Life of Katharine Hepburn.* New York: Norton, 1975.

Kanin, Garson. *Tracy and Hepburn: An Intimate Memoir.* New York: Viking Press, 1971.

Leaming, Barbara. *Katharine Hepburn.* New York: Crown Publishers, 1995.

Mann, William J. *Kate: The Woman Who Was Hepburn.* New York: Henry Holt and Company, 2006.

Morley, Sheridan. *Katharine Hepburn: A Celebration.* London: Pavilion Books, 1984.

Parish, James Robert. *Katharine Hepburn: The Untold Story.* New York: Advocate Books, 2005.

Prideaux, James. *Knowing Hepburn and Other Curious Experiences.* Boston: Faber and Faber, 1996.

AND OTHERS

George Cukor

Lambert, Gavin. *On Cukor.* New York: Rizzoli, 2000.

Levy, Emanuel. *George Cukor, Master of Elegance: Hollywood's Legendary Director and His Stars.* New York: William Morrow, 1994.

Bernardoni, James. *George Cukor: A Critical Study and Filmography.* Jefferson, North Carolina: McFarland, 1985.

Howard Hawks

Hillier, Jim, and Peter Wollen, eds. *Howard Hawks: American Artist.* London: British Film Institute, 1997.

Mast, Gerald. *Howard Hawks, Storyteller.* New York: Oxford University Press, 1982.

McCarthy, Todd. *Howard Hawks: The Grey Fox of Hollywood.* New York: Grove Press, 1997.

Howard Hughes
Brown, Peter Harry, and Pat H. Broeske. *Howard Hughes: The Untold Story.* New York: Da Capo Press, 1996.
Drosnin, Michael. *Citizen Hughes: The Power, the Money and the Madness.* New York: Broadway (Reprint Edition), 2004.

Spencer Tracy
Davidson, Bill. *Spencer Tracy: Tragic Idol.* New York: Dutton, 1988.
Swindells, Larry. *Spencer Tracy.* New York: World Publishing Company, 1969.

GENERAL HOLLYWOOD HISTORY

Haskell, Molly. *From Reverence to Rape: The Treatment of Women in the Movies.* Chicago: University of Chicago Press, 1987.
Mast, Gerald. *A Short History of the* Movies, 9th edition. New York: Longman, 2005.
Stevens, George, Jr., ed. *Conversations with the Great Moviemakers of Hollywood's Golden Age at the American Film Institute.* New York: Alfred A. Knopf, 2006.

A NOTE ON THE AUTHOR

Karen Karbo is the author of three novels, all of which were named *New York Times* Notable Books. Her most recent work, *The Stuff of Life: A Daughter's Memoir*, was a selection of the Satellite Sisters Radio Book Club and won the Oregon Book Award for Creative Nonfiction. A past winner of the General Electric Foundation Award for Younger Writers, Karen is in addition the recipient of a grant from the National Endowment for the Arts. Her essays, reviews, and articles have appeared in the *New York Times*, *Redbook*, *Elle*, *Vogue*, *Esquire*, *Outside*, and *More*. She lives in Portland, Oregon. Her favorite Hepburn movie is *Holiday*.